CONNECTION

The Discovery of a Soul System

CONNECTION

The Discovery of a Soul System

Brough Perkins
John Topp

IGUANA

Copyright @ 2021 Brough Perkins and John Topp
Published by Iguana Books
720 Bathurst Street, Suite 303
Toronto, ON M5S 2R4

All rights reserved. No part of this publication may be reproduced, stored in a retrieval system or transmitted, in any form or by any means, electronic, mechanical, recording or otherwise (except brief passages for purposes of review) without the prior permission of the author.

Publisher: Meghan Behse
Editor: Lee Parpart
Front cover design: Meghan Behse

ISBN 978-1-77180-473-8 (paperback)
ISBN 978-1-77180-474-5 (epub)

This is an original print edition of *Connection: The Discovery of a Soul System*.

Table of Contents

Where Two or More Are Gathered 1
I'm Aware of a Presence 33
All in Small 42
Growth and Evolution 59
With the Current 73
The Highest Form of Light 99
Contacting Your Guide 120
Blinded by the Light 138
Cohesive Thinking 175
The Ancient Art of True Blessing 222
The Origins of Guilt 235
The Duality of Progression and Regression 249

Presentiments are strange things! and so are sympathies; and so are signs; and the three combined make one mystery to which humanity has not yet found the key. I never laughed at presentiments in my life, because I have had strange ones of my own. Sympathies, I believe, exist (for instance, between far-distant, long-absent, wholly estranged relatives asserting, notwithstanding their alienation, the unity of the source to which each traces his origin) whose workings baffle mortal comprehension. And signs, for aught we know, may be but the sympathies of Nature with man.

— Charlotte Brontë, *Jane Eyre*

Where Two or More Are Gathered

This is a story about friendship, connection, and the nature of reality. It involves psychic ability, startling coincidences, and mysterious voices and photographs, culminating in what is known in spiritual and New Age circles as "channelling," or the use of the mind and body as a vehicle for another mind that is not located in this physical world.

In late 2015, Brough Perkins, my friend and professional psychic medium, and I attempted channelling and found a consciousness distinct from our own, ready and willing to communicate messages of depth and wisdom to the world, through us.

We relate these experiences as plainly as possible, without exaggeration or enhancement, and with the understanding that no one is expected to simply believe they are true or agree with our interpretation of them. The bulk of the book consists of verbatim transcripts of our recorded channelling sessions. The rest describes the circumstances that led up to these encounters and the discussions and events surrounding them. We offer this supporting material to help the reader understand (at least as much as we understand) how this channel opened up, what processes we followed in receiving and presenting the content of the channelling, and our thoughts and feelings as the project progressed. We include photos for this same reason, and we will provide audio and video excerpts through the web.

Through these different media, anyone who is interested in paranormal experience and in our encounters can form their own view of what is happening here. Some readers — for example, those who have had similar experiences — may not have trouble believing our account. For those who are agnostic, skeptical, or disbelieving, we invite your scrutiny and engagement and ask only that you keep an open mind.

One way to engage with this book is to keep an eye out for unusual things that may happen in your life or in connection with the material we present here while you are reading it. Another is to simply make the decision to suspend disbelief until the end. The spirit of this project is not one of detached observation, but of participation. Try to let go of preconceptions and allow yourself to connect with the message that comes through in these transcripts. As we are told later on, "Paranormal phenomena, as you'd call it — synchronicity, psychic phenomena — all point toward oneness." In this oneness, all of our experiences are connected.

* * *

Brough Perkins has been a working psychic medium since his teens and has performed thousands of readings for clients ranging from individuals to police departments. Brough has been featured on Canadian television and radio, and was included in a W5 episode on CTV as a more authentic counterpoint to a number of dishonest psychics who were exposed in this investigative piece. He was one of five psychics tested in the book *Medium7: Evidence of the Afterlife and Predictions* by criminologist Donna Smith-Moncrieffe, which concludes that the mediums tested, including Brough, were getting information — accurate information — from non-physical sources.

Through fifteen years of being a close friend to Brough, I have seen his abilities at work first-hand many times. I've become familiar with the look of quiet focus that comes across his face, his head tilted down slightly, eyes squinted, as he receives and relays data that he has no earthly way of knowing. The second time I met him in person, we were out for a drink and he spontaneously described the detailed circumstances in which I met my partner at the time, before knowing much of anything about me or her. In a recent reading over the phone, Brough's client didn't ask him anything about health, but he informed her that he saw calcium deposits forming in her breast tissue, and that they were not dangerous. She then told him that she'd had a mammogram the week previous, and the doctor identified calcium deposits, and told her they are considered harmless. I have been present in the room for at least a dozen phone readings where he has identified names of relatives, specific medical conditions, and detailed career information that was then verified by his client. He can do it over the phone, he can do it over a beer, he can do it on live radio and television, and the accuracy is often so startling that people ask, "How do you know that?" to which he answers, "I'm psychic." I have no doubt in my mind that Brough possesses highly developed psychic ability.

Brough grew up in the Pierrefonds suburb of Montreal. His father was so into biking that he named his son after the WWI-period Brough Superior motorcycle made in England. In the UK this name is pronounced to rhyme with "rough," but he pronounces it "Bro." From an early age, Brough had unusual experiences, such as precognitive dreams, and visitations from his grandfather who had recently passed away. At times the face of a woman would appear behind his eyelids, taking shape out of abstract forms. When he opened his eyes, he could still see her face, appearing as though it was projected on a wall. In his mind he heard her name as "Sharon," and she would appear on a regular basis.

In fourth grade he noticed a pink light around his teacher. He felt himself going into a trance, "which feels like your brain is being tickled and you're just staring." The words "you're having a baby" fell out of his mouth. The teacher explained to Brough in front of the class that she had just found out that day that she was pregnant, after trying to conceive for fourteen years.

Young Brough

The following year on the way home from school, Brough had a vision of the side door to the house being open, accompanied by a feeling of urgency. He ran home and found the side door open. Inside, his sister's friend, Ryan, was having a seizure brought on by an asthma attack. Brough enlisted the help of a neighbour who happened to have a nebulizer that delivered asthma medication, which saved Ryan.

After this incident, Brough was seen by friends and family as someone with special abilities, and more importantly, he began to recognize this as part of who he was. But despite this new openness with himself and others about his abilities, the prospect of starting high school and trying to find his place in the world was too much. Brough began to experience mental and physical symptoms of depression.

At age fifteen, Brough's family moved to Mississauga, Ontario, which meant leaving behind his friends and cousins. Brough started ninth grade and soon dropped out because of anxiety. His parents got him into an alternative school where he had a later start and could work at his own pace. At school he met Laura, a fellow goth who, like him, was also interested in the paranormal.

While living in Mississauga, Brough got in the habit of watching DVDs of live concerts in the basement when he came home after school. "One day I was doing a weird little dance by myself in the basement with this concert on. Out of the blue I had a very clear vision of Sharon, the woman I used to see, projected onto the wall in my bedroom. She was clapping at me, like she was applauding. And I was like, 'What?' And then I felt embarrassed, and I turned off the DVD and left the basement."

Visions and precognitive dreams continued sporadically. He ate up *Unsolved Mysteries* and *Ghostbusters*, and discovered Art Bell's paranormal-themed program *Coast to Coast AM* on late-night radio. He discovered the psychic Sylvia Browne on *The Montel Williams Show* and learned about the concept of a spirit guide through her books and appearances. The idea was that everyone had one, although they normally weren't conscious of it. One day with Laura and some friends, Brough, out loud, asked his spirit guide to turn on a lamp. Nothing happened and everyone had a chuckle. Then after a minute, the lamp turned on. One of his friends said, "I saw it, but I don't believe it."

Once again it was time to move, this time to Richmond Hill, Ontario. Once again, this meant leaving friends and going back to a regular high school, where Brough dropped out. He was hitting rock bottom. "I'm feeling completely useless with life. I've failed everything," he explained. "I collected all the pills I could find. Sleeping pills. I was in the bathroom ready to down them all." At that moment he heard a woman's voice next to him. She said, "Honey, honey, honey, my name is Laron."

"It was physically real," Brough remembers. "I think that if someone else had been there, they would have heard it. It was like she was right here floating. I was so terrified that I ran out of the house. I ran down to the park and started crying, releasing all this emotion." He knew right away that this was the woman he had been calling "Sharon." She was announcing herself to him, and making clear her name. The memories of the psychic events throughout his life flashed to him: his grandfather, the pregnant teacher with the pink aura, Ryan's asthma attack. Until then, those were isolated incidents. Laron pulled them together and showed him the bigger picture about who he was.

This direct contact with someone who seemed to be a spirit guide startled Brough out of suicidal thoughts and gave him a sense of comfort. He also started to think that life after death was a likely thing, in which case, suicide didn't seem like an escape from problems.

Brough's father found a suicide note Brough had written before Laron's visit. He took Brough out for lunch and explained to him that high school isn't the only way to succeed in life. His uncle Danny was a self-made millionaire and never started high school. He told Brough to take some time off without any pressure. They would revisit school when the time was right. "The problem was I felt like a huge failure, so this 'permission slip' was very important to me."

Brough felt guided to change everything. "My job was to wake up, stop listening to dark goth music, and start focusing on positive things. This will sound stupid, but I watched *Touched by An Angel*. I'd go to Chapters and find spiritual books."

For the first time, Brough sought out people for whom he could do psychic readings. He found internet chat rooms dedicated to the subject of psychic work. He impressed one girl named Kelly, who turned out to live in Aurora, next door to Richmond Hill, even though most people in the chat were from the US. Kelly and Brough became friends in real life, and she took him to her high school and introduced him around. A crowd of students gathered around him in the cafeteria and he gave them readings. One guy started crying. "I was starting to reconstruct a worldview where spirit is real, and light and good have a valid place."

Laron continued to talk to him. She told him, "The first step is to take down the mental blocks you have built to repress your natural gift."

Brough said, "What do you mean, what mental blocks?"

She replied, "All of your false beliefs."

Brough told me, "And with that message flooded into my mind all of the times where, you know, your parent loses their temper with you, but you interpret that forever as you being not good enough, or society telling you that you're not a real person and you have to create yourself."

He would have moments of vivid realization, similar to when he was younger and lying on the couch and having hyper-awareness. "Now I was wearing light-coloured clothing, meditating. It took three days — each day I woke up, I felt significantly happier. I was seeing sparks of light, having Kundalini-like love feelings." (In Hinduism, Kundalini refers to energy associated with the divine feminine.) "Love would flow out of me. Within three days I was cured of all depression. It had been deep for three years, like there wasn't anywhere lower to go."

His new realization was that if light is all that there is, and if darkness is an absence of light, then darkness, when it exists in us, is due to a blockage. He was taking down false beliefs and replacing them with true beliefs. "You're psychic, you're a loving soul, and the reason you're so angry is because you love so much — your anger is like a call for love. So something snapped in me and I realized, I am only love. And the things that are not love about me are not really me."

He decided he needed to get a job and stay active to keep his momentum going. He thought a bookstore might work. He mentally received the information: "On main street in town there's a shop." He walked around and found a spiritual New Age place called Where Angels Gather. Gloria, the owner, gave him a job and said he could use a room in the back of the store to do readings.

Brough's mother had given him a film camera before moving from Mississauga. He took some pictures of himself with his friends before leaving high school, then left the camera sitting around for a year. He decided to get the film developed. On picking it up, the clerk explained that the film had been exposed to light and that most of the pictures had been wiped out. Brough didn't understand how that could have happened since he used the film normally and had done nothing to expose it to light. He took the pictures home and had a look.

Of the 24 pictures, about the first 20 were just white because they'd been exposed to light. A couple of pictures from the end of the roll came through normally. However, in between, just after the white pictures, there was a picture that was mostly black. In the top-right corner were three small squares arranged horizontally. In the bottom-left corner there was a woman in a blue shirt and glasses, smiling. Her hands were together as though she was clapping, the camera capturing her right at the point of her hands connecting. She was lit as though there was a spotlight on her, bringing her into sharp relief against the dark background.

A woman appears on Brough's roll of film.

Brough knew he had not taken this picture, but he did recognize the image. It was Laron, who had appeared in his mind a year before, clapping.

"It was mind-boggling because I know exactly what I did with the camera. It was specifically used to take some pictures at high school of my friends before I left Mississauga. And then a couple photos of myself. There was nothing that I did with that camera that could result in that picture. And I had been seeing her mentally, and I suppose you could call them apparitions. So, I was seeing her, and here she was on a physical roll of film.

"It was big, because I had no experience giving readings. Later on, when doing readings, I would say to the client, 'Your dead father's name is Ralph,' and the client would verify that information as being true. But at the time, I had nothing like that in my life to verify my experiences; they were all internal experiences, like, 'I had this dream and it came true but nobody knows.' Sylvia Browne was popular and I'd heard tell of psychics. But I was like, 'Am I one? 'Cause I'm not doing what Sylvia does.' So, the Laron picture solidified it for me. And I got the mental sense from her that that's what the picture was for."

When he received the image of Laron clapping in his mind, the camera was present in the house. Brough believes that the image was simultaneously transmitted to two destinations: one mental and one physical. "Hers was at the tail end of the exposed frames. And you'll see there is some light exposure on the picture, at the bottom. So I think it was a burst of spirit energy that did that to the photos."

The image is definitely unusual. Her image is simply *there* in stark clarity against the blackness. Below the shoulders, the image is cut off in a straight line at a slight angle. Some of Brough's friends have said this looks like someone might have taken a picture of a television screen. The problem is that there is no sign of a television. The image stands alone.

The squares at the top right resemble stage lights or windows in a movie theatre where the light of the projector shines through. Combined with the appearance of the woman being lit by a spotlight, the two elements could be seen as intentionally combined. But the most remarkable part of the image is the blurred clapping hands, caught at the point of contact. To get that precision, you would probably have to take a rapid series of frames and then choose the one where the hands meet. But this was a single photo.

Brough had reconnected with a teacher from high school. Her daughter, Amanda Walsh, had become a host on the popular Canadian television channel MuchMusic. She heard that Brough was going to investigate a haunted house in Goderich, Ontario and suggested they make a Hallowe'en special out of it. Brough was interested in media work and was excited to see where this might lead.

Brough on Much Music in 2008.

On the show, Brough and Amanda walked around the house with the camera crew, and he picked up impressions about the house's history. He named the original owner of the house, which they later verified. The first showing had half a million viewers, making it one of the most popular shows they had done. Brough's email address was given, and he received over a thousand emails in the first hour and many more later. Over three years he answered each one.

This opportunity led to regular appearances on mainstream television and radio over the next few years. Brough was comfortable with a big audience. He could keep his charm and sense of humour while displaying his abilities during a live broadcast. The media work, along with word-of-mouth referrals, gave him a steady stream of people looking for readings.

Brough became friends with one of his clients, Anita. They would see each other every day. Around this time Brough noticed something strange. He was seeing the numbers 22 or 222 a lot in everyday life — on clocks, licence plates, and receipts that would often come to $2.22 or $22.22. He wasn't in the habit of noticing numbers, so this pattern of 2s stood out in sharp relief. Then one day Anita said to him, "I've been having this weird thing with seeing the number 222."

This continued for both of them for a few months. Brough remembers seeing the number everywhere. "You'd never think you'd be getting sick of a number. It was more than pattern recognition because it was coming *at* you." Anita pressed Brough to figure out the meaning of this pattern, so he set his mind to it. "I woke up one morning with this inspired thought that came out of nowhere. That there needs to be an organization of some kind that can act as Starfleet Command, but for this internal dimensional exploration — inner space instead of outer space. Since I'm a *Star Trek* fan, it was put into that framework because that's the language I would understand."

The acronym "ARC" showed up in his mind, which then translated to Afterlife Research Centre. "The arc shape has that sense of being a bridge; it's a symbol of interconnectedness, so it's an institution of exploration, research, and discovery, and also acts as a central hub or database for all relevant information in this field. That came to me." It also came to him that, through ARC, he would be introduced to others of a similar mindset.

* * *

My role in this story could be seen as that of an instigator, coordinator, witness, producer, or all of the above. While Brough's life is squarely and overtly in the realm of the paranormal, down to his very livelihood, I have always lived in two worlds. In one, I'm a father, digital technologist working for big corporations, guitar player, vegetarian, and cyclist. In the other world, which runs in parallel to my daily world, I see the world of experience as a medium of communication involving constant synchronicities, precognitive dreams, and telepathic intuitions. Since my early twenties, I have seen the outer world and the conscious mind not as self-contained, distinct phenomena, but as layers within a deeper set of stratifications that transcend physical laws. The physical laws are the product of something else — something we can perceive only indirectly, in glimpses and intuitions. Whereas Brough receives information mentally, which is to say, psychically, I receive information through interpreting events in the external world and exploring the way they intersect with thoughts and dreams, with reference to a kind of super-order that exists in and around the conventional order. To me, paranormal phenomena such as UFOs, crop circles, and synchronicities are all manifestations of this super-order. I am drawn to this frontier where mind and environment are one. Maybe this is why I'm given, as you'll see, the title "psychic technician."

John's early interest in synchronicity.

After high school, I shunned all learning institutions and anything resembling a career because I didn't want to be entangled in what I saw as the mainstream world. I earned a minimum of money at simple jobs and rejected my university acceptance in order to stay connected with the other world that I perceived. But this didn't go anywhere; I was putting off finding my place in the world and not really connecting with either the mainstream or the other world. Once I embraced life and became engaged, both sides became more enriched. I moved in with my girlfriend, Carmen, and started a new career in web development. While on one hand I feared that my link to the world of spirit would be severed,

I discovered that this other world was reaching into my life through dreams, synchronicities, and musical inspiration. I continued to explore this side of life while developing my relationship and jumping headfirst into the working world. I found that these two worlds fed and inspired each other if some balance was maintained between them.

One phenomenon — synchronicity — became the force that would change the course of my life and Brough's. Carl Jung coined the term "synchronicity" to describe the experience of external events aligning with thoughts or dreams in a way that cannot be explained by conventional ideas about causality. In *Synchronicity: An Acausal Connecting Principle*, Jung relates that his first obvious experience of this phenomenon took place during a psychotherapy session with a patient. She was describing a dream she had had of a scarab beetle when a scarab beetle flew in the open window. He picked it up, presented it to her, and said, "Madame, there is your scarab."

John in his twenties.

I began to experience occasional synchronicities in my mid-twenties, and I responded with wonder to these episodes of alignment between my thoughts and the external world. I suspect that as children we experience synchronicity but don't notice it, because we haven't yet formed firm distinctions between the inner and outer worlds. In my late twenties these synchronicities took on a detailed precision, as if going from low definition to high definition, and I began to perceive themes in the threads that were woven together, like clues for me to follow.

The first detailed case of this happened while I was walking in downtown Toronto with Carmen. She remarked out of the blue that she had been hearing the name Jasmine a lot. She gave a few examples, the main one being a character from the television show *Angel*, a spin-off of *Buffy the Vampire Slayer*. The character of Jasmine, also known as The Blessed Devourer, was a member of a group of ancient beings known as The Powers That Be. According to the Buffyverse website, The Powers That Be referred to "the first beings to exist in the Earth dimension after the schism that created them and the Old Ones [*demons*]." After leaving this dimension, "these beings watched over mankind and guided the forces of good."

Seconds after Carmen explained this, we approached a small group of people who had binoculars and were very busy watching something and taking notes. We asked them what they were doing, and they told us they were watching some kind of rare hawk that was passing through the city and had set up a nest high up on the side of a tower. As we talked, they mentioned that they had named the bird Jasmine.

Similar things would happen sporadically. For example, I began to notice strange patterns, such as seeing the letter S all the time. Often this would not be an actual printed letter, but an object taking on an S-form. For example, I would see a hair in the sink or the tub shaped like an S. Not once or twice, but frequently for a period, and then not at all. I had no desire or need to see S-shapes everywhere, and no way to know what they meant.

Other strange things that seemed to be overtly paranormal started happening as well. One day while at work, I picked up a message on my cellphone from an unidentified caller. It sounded like overhearing a conversation between two men in a place with a lot of echo. The way they spoke was as if they were from a different time, maybe the 1950s. It went on for a while, and I couldn't make out most of what they said. Then I heard one of them say, "John Topp" and then "trying to understand human suffering." I played it to my co-worker, and he heard the same words and found the whole sound of it very strange. At some level I knew this was not normal. There seemed to be a part of me that *knew* when something abnormal was happening and was not surprised by it, as if I knew where it came from.

In 2004, while we were expecting our first daughter, Carmen and I went to the hospital for an orientation session. They showed us the type of room Carmen would stay in after the birth. I was in full dad mode, taking pictures of everything, including the bathroom adjoining the maternity room. Looking at the shots later, I noticed something unusual in the bathroom photo. My reflection was in the mirror, and over my right shoulder was the face of a woman wearing glasses and a white earring. Because the camera was designed to be held below you with the tiny screen facing up, I am looking down, so I wouldn't have seen anything in the mirror. No one of that description or any other had been in the room with us. Carmen and I had been alone, and it wasn't Carmen. It didn't look like her, and other photos of Carmen from that same set clearly show her with different hair, no glasses, and no white earring. The face in the photo was strangely perched just over my shoulder as if it was a photo-bomb. I could tell it was something unusual, but I filed it away and didn't think much more about it at the time.

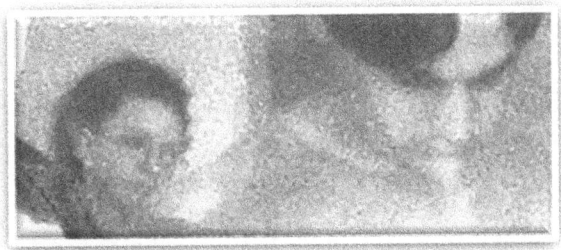

Close-up of John's photo with an unidentified woman appearing next to him. Enhanced for clarity.

By now the internet had become widely used. Through it, I was able to go deeper into my interest in the paranormal. I found websites on UFOs, crop circles, and cryptids. I was especially interested in the idea of information being obtained through channelling. Channelling refers to a situation where a person goes into a trance state and allows a non-corporeal entity of some kind to come through their consciousness in order to communicate a message, usually by speaking or writing. This is different from possession, which is seen as a spirit occupying a person's body uninvited, against the host's will, and not for the purpose of conveying coherent information. Channelling is deliberate and planned, with the aim of obtaining information from outside of this world.

In May 2005, I began to experience a new, steady flow of synchronicities. They happened almost daily. Since I didn't perceive them as random, it stood to reason that *someone* must have created them. It also seemed that these events would not be trivial to create. It seemed wrong to let them go unrecorded — like throwing away works of art. So, I started a blog.

The first episode I blogged about was the Jasmine one — the synchronicity between the *Angel* episode and the bird. I documented each new synchronicity when it happened, usually every day or two. As they continued, a pattern emerged across the synchronicities. I posted:

> A few days ago I was reading a book on geometry … I read about the Pythagorean theorem, which states that the two short sides of a right-angle triangle will give you the length of the long side, using the equation
>
> $$a^2+b^2=c^2$$
>
> I remembered it from school and I thought, as I sometimes do, "Well, if I was on *Jeopardy* and that came up, I'd be prepared."
>
> The next day, Carmen was watching *Jeopardy* and for one of the questions up pops a right-angle triangle with the short sides given as 30 and 35. Challenge was to give the length of the long side. I didn't get the answer right.

Some friends and family found the blog interesting, and readers started noticing synchronicities happening with them as well, sometimes tying into the ones I was experiencing. I called them "field reporters" and would include their reports in my blog posts. One of my field reporters was my co-worker Stephanie. A week after the Pythagorean-theorem post, Stephanie asked me if I knew of someone who could babysit for a friend of hers. Her friend was Jacob Richler, son of Canadian author Mordecai Richler, who wrote a well-known children's book called *Jacob Two-Two Meets the Hooded Fang*. The hero, Jacob, is a kid based on the real-life Jacob.

In the book, Jacob Two-Two earns his name from a perceived defect acquired from being the littlest member of his family. Because he's the youngest, people often don't hear what he's saying, so he gets into the habit of saying everything twice. He also expresses numbers by adding twos together: "I am two plus two plus two years old." He has two brothers and two sisters. At the corner store he asks for "two quarts of chocolate ice cream please, two quarts of chocolate ice cream please." When his repetition leads to a misunderstanding that lands him in prison, the judge sentences him to "two months, two days, two hours, two minutes in the darkest dungeons of prison."

A couple of days after Stephanie asked me to help find a babysitter for Jacob Richler, my mother emailed me. She had been at one of the University of Toronto libraries within an hour or two of when Stephanie made that request, and she (my mom) found a synchronicity in the stacks.

> I was in the Victoria College library on Thursday, at closing time, and a harried young student was at the checkout desk in front of me, anxiously trying to track down a copy of Joseph Heller's *Catch-22*. The librarian sent her off to Trinity College where she thought she might find a copy. I came back to the apartment, settled down for tea and a read of the newly arrived *New Yorker*, and opened it at random to a poem by Kurt Vonnegut on ... Joseph Heller and *Catch-22*...

My mother then proceeded to quote, in full, the poem "True story, Word of Honor," which tells the story of a meeting between Vonnegut and Heller at a party hosted by a billionaire on Shelter Island. Describing Heller as "an important and funny writer / now dead," the poem goes on to recount a wry anecdote about the comparative wealth of Heller and the billionaire. Vonnegut asks Heller how it feels to know that their party host made more money in one day than *Catch-22* earned in its entire history, and Heller replies that he has something the billionaire will never have: "The knowledge that I've got enough." This poem has been circulated widely on the internet and is sometimes read at Thanksgiving, as a testament to the virtues of gratitude and simplicity.

My mother had this synchronicity involving *Catch-22* before I had started to recognize a 22 pattern. The Pythagorean episode was interesting unto itself, but it wasn't until later that I noticed the formula $a^2+b^2=c^2$ contained three 2s. Between *Jacob Two-Two*, *Catch-22*, and the formula, I started to see the pattern. This was then cemented when Stephanie told me she was currently reading *Catch-22*.

The numeral 2 started appearing in other places too. I had been troubled by a hernia for a couple of years, and my doctor had booked me into the Hernia Hilton, also known as Shouldice Hospital in Toronto, where people come from around the world to have their hernias repaired. Robin Williams had been there a couple of weeks prior.

They gave me room 228. Each room was shared by two people. And all of the objects in the rooms were labelled with either a 1 or a 2. The nurse told me, "Anything labelled '2' is yours." My bed, my half of the closet, my bathroom drawer and towel holder were all labelled with the number 2.

I realized there was a strong theme of the numbers 2 or 22 coming through in multiple areas of my life, starting with the Pythagorean theorem and becoming more obvious after that.

While 0 is a non-number, 1 is the only number representing a single unit, and 2 is the first number of plurality, or multiplicity. The glyph used in Western languages for the number 2 evolved from the Brahmic script, the basis for languages in India and parts of Asia. It started as two horizontal lines, like an equal sign. And 2 is considered a good number in Chinese culture — there is a Chinese saying, "Good things come in pairs."

I felt like I was receiving a communication. This was of course interesting, but also unsettling. I didn't know why it was happening, but I felt as if a mind was speaking to me, and I wanted to know who this mind was.

* * *

While all of this was going on, one of my "field reporters," Natasha Kong, who was following the blog and having her own synchronicities tying into mine, was working at the CBC. She was a producer for *The Nerve*, a television and web series with an edgy youth demographic. They had an episode in the works about the paranormal, and Natasha was doing research for it. She found one of Brough's MuchMusic appearances and contacted him to be interviewed for the show. Intrigued by his personality and abilities, she booked a reading with him.

During the reading, Brough was getting messages from Natasha's grandfather. Her grandfather was showing him a number: 22. As he was in his phase of seeing the number everywhere, he thought this related to him personally and didn't bother to bring it up as part of the reading. Then he looked at the clock and it showed 7:22. That's when he decided to mention it.

He said to Natasha, "You have a connection to the number 22. I think you might know somebody." Natasha replied, "That's specifically correct, and it's such an unusual thing for you to even bring up." She told him about my blog and how I had noticed the theme of the numbers 22 and 222 in the synchronicities I was experiencing.

On June 6, 2015, two weeks after I wrote my blog post about these numbers, I received an email from Brough Perkins with the subject "A sign." In the email, he explained how he came to find me and said, "I have information for you about the signs you've been receiving from the other side." He told me that he and his friend Anita had been seeing the numbers 2 and 22 everywhere since January of that year. He explained that they were starting the Afterlife Research Centre (ARC), with the directive to "explore the unknown and higher dimensional spirit realms as well as change the state of the planet through altruism and selflessness toward all beings." He said that he had been made aware psychically that through synchronicity he would meet others to work with him in this mission.

This boggled my mind. Even if one thinks that Brough and I were both deluded in thinking this number had any sort of significance and that it was just a matter of each of us looking for patterns, there is still the problem that *both* of us were identifying the pattern at the same time, and that we were then *connected* as a result of this. We eventually concluded that the 2s and 22s were acting as a beacon — a signal woven into the flow of experience, drawing us toward each other.

I read Brough's email many times. It had an almost science-fiction quality to it: the Afterlife Research Centre. But he wrote passionately, and I had the feeling that Brough and Anita were experiencing something genuine, and that we needed to meet. The deciding factor was our shared experience with patterns around the numbers 2 and 22, which seemed to be coming from a source that was grander than any of us.

I replied to Brough and we then chatted online. I noticed right away that I felt as if I knew him. He was serious in tone, but I just wanted to throw jokes at him right from the beginning. He started to respond to them right away and return the humour. There was a chemistry there, present from before we met in person, that would continue throughout our relationship.

A couple of weeks after talking online, Brough and Anita came to our house for a visit. He was tall, thin, and handsome, with prominent cheekbones and a bit of teenage acne. He wore a bandana around his head. Anita was a pretty, young South Asian woman who hid behind an oversized hockey jersey and usually had a cigarette lit.

My daughter was about ten months old at the time of this visit, and I handed her to Brough to hold. He was terrified, having never held a baby. But as he later told me, he took this as a sign of immediate trust.

Over the following weeks we met, phoned, and emailed, and developed our ideas about what was going on. About a week before meeting me, Brough had heard an Art Bell radio show about something called "instrumental transcommunication," or ITC. The term refers to a documented phenomenon from the last few decades of unidentified voices coming through devices such as tape recorders and radios, as well as unidentified images coming through television sets.

John and Brough meet.

During one of our conversations about instrumental transcommunication, Brough showed me the photograph he had of a woman clapping — the one that had appeared on his exposed roll of film when he was a teenager. He explained to me that this was Laron, his spirit guide. The photo was very unusual; the woman appeared with nothing in the background, smiling, her hands connecting in mid-clap, the three lights resembling movie- projector windows above her. I showed him the digital photo I had from a year earlier in the hospital, when an unidentified woman showed up over my shoulder. Fast-forward to years later — during the production of this book — while looking at the hospital photo, the thought suddenly took hold of me: Are these women in the photographs the same person? I zoomed. I cropped. I changed brightness and contrast. The faces looked similar in eyes, nose, and mouth. The graininess of my photo made it hard to tell, but it seemed like they were wearing a similar pair of glasses. There was what looked like a white earring on her right ear in my photo, on her left ear in Brough's. Each had a necklace. Only bangs were visible in Brough's photo, but the hair appeared dark in both, although differently styled. The eyebrows in both were thin and manicured.

I checked the date my photo was taken: June 6, 2004. I didn't know of any significance to that. It was about a year before Brough first emailed me, but I had always thought of us meeting in May. I went back and checked the email: June 6, 2005. Did Laron appear in my photo one year to the day before I met Brough? The more I look at the photos side by side, the more I believe that this is what happened.

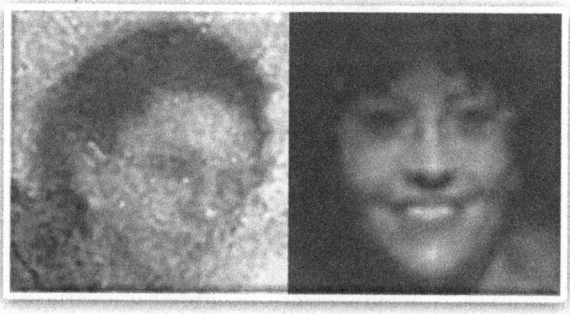

Comparison of the woman that appeared in John's and Brough's photos.

* * *

The most commonly known type of instrumental transcommunication is electronic voice phenomenon, or EVP, which is the presence of voices of unknown origin on audio recordings. Brough told me that he had tried some experiments with EVP and got what sounded like faint voices in the hiss of the audio. I had heard of EVP years before but thought it would just be hours of listening to static with, likely, no results, so I didn't think of trying it. It was one of those things that seemed too good to be true, to have that kind of direct contact with spirits through technology. The fact that Brough had a result changed my perspective completely, and I turned my attention toward this most strange phenomenon.

EVP is very simple to try but not necessarily easy to get results with. You just take an audio-recording device, like a tape recorder or a laptop or a portable digital recorder, and record in a quiet room. You leave it recording for a few minutes, then listen back. When listening back, you turn the volume way up, which increases what's called the "noise floor" of the recording, which is just the white noise that is always in the background. Within that hiss you may hear voices or sounds that don't seem like they would be from the surroundings and were not audible during the recording.

I first tried it by recording through the microphone on my laptop. My experience with digital audio came in handy; I would take samples of recordings or sounds I found and amplify, reverse, or speed them up or slow them down, and so on. I turned the microphone up to full and recorded maybe ten minutes of sound. I played back the file, maximizing the signal so I was listening to loud white noise through my headphones. Every movement I made during the recording was amplified; you could hear the fabric of my clothes, and if I moved the laptop, it was deafening. With my headphones on at top volume, there was an intensity to listening back to just *air*.

After several minutes of listening to every shuffle, click, sigh, and sniffle, I heard a sound which seemed alien to everything else. It was like a low male vocal sound, like a grunt. If it had been my own voice it would have been very loud. But this was *inside* the static, or emerging from it. Then a minute later, the same kind of voice — but now sounding like it was singing in baritone. These didn't seem like voices that could be from the neighbours, coming through the wall. I continued doing this on a regular basis and would get fragments of voice showing up almost every time. After a few more tries, I had a very clear adult female voice show up. It seemed to be saying, "Let's talk, John." This same voice would appear throughout many of my recordings. Later, another voice came through even more clearly, this time saying the words "in spirit." The name Penelope turned up in the recordings more than once, and I came to associate the name with this female voice. Brough and I started to refer to Penelope as my spirit guide, in the same way that Laron was his spirit guide.

This became a form of meditation and focus for me. I learned how my state of mind affected how successful the attempt would be. There was a process of tuning in. I tried to get information through EVP. In one case I tried to contact my friend's deceased father, whose name was Anthony. I asked out loud to speak to Anthony. Listening back to the recording, I heard a voice saying, "My name's just Tony." I relayed this to my friend, and she told me that he went by Tony. In another case I did a recording for a friend of Brough's and received a last name that was his mother's maiden name. Brough said that the way I was getting information was very similar to how it came through to him when he was doing a reading for someone. So in my own way I was developing a form of mediumship. Over two years I amassed hundreds of audio clips of unexplained voices. Even if someone might explain them away by saying they are stray radio signals or voices leaking into the house from outside, it's hard to explain how I had a crystal-clear female voice saying, "in spirit," completely out of the blue.

During this period, I had a series of dreams that were charged with significance and left me feeling that something very important had been communicated. In one dream, I was in a boat on the water with a group of younger, progressive, future-facing people. The boat was stationary, floating. From a distance, a giant cruise ship approached. On the deck of the ship were giant figures, standing storeys high. They didn't all appear at once, though; there was a kind of space they would walk through and become visible one after the other, as though invisible curtains were being opened on a stage. As the ship approached, I got out of the boat. I held up a staff that looked like a giant Q-tip, with soft material at each end. Just as the ship was going to make contact with the boat, I held the staff between the two to prevent a collision.

With the arrival of our second daughter, we were a family of four. My girls were, and still are, the world to me. While I was sleep deprived at times, their energy boosted and inspired me. I kept every bit of artwork, wrote down their spontaneous weird phrases in my notebooks (once my oldest proclaimed, "There is a big god and a little god, and the little god is all the things we see around us like the trees and the flowers") and made voice recordings of their songs. They formed a band called Psychic Palm Readers, with no prompting from me or Brough on the name. My youngest was the main songwriter, with titles such as "Lightning Is Gravity" and "I Don't Like It When My Jacket Is Zipped Up."

As I slowed down on the EVP work in 2007, I started writing for an online magazine called *Reality Sandwich*. I wrote a piece about ITC that generated a lot of discussion in the comments section. Further waves of synchronicities hit me as I got involved in this online community, some involving other writers for the magazine, in a similar way to what happened with field reporters for my blog. I wrote a piece called "The Book in the Sky" that followed this journey, which involved symbolism of the capital letter A appearing in the sky. The letter had appeared in dreams had by both me and a fellow writer within the same month. This symbolism appearing to two people indicated to me that this was information being conveyed from a source outside of us, and our job was to try to understand these symbols. Through some connections afforded by these synchronicities, I interpreted the main message of the two dreams, mine and my colleague's, as being imminent accessibility to information that was previously hidden.

* * *

In this same year, Brough moved out of his parents' place in the suburbs and into his own apartment downtown. He also rented an office through a client, where he did readings. He was building his business and enjoying his independence. I was seeing a little more of him since he was so much closer. His first media appearance on MuchMusic had led to more appearances on television and radio, which helped him build a steady clientele. I listened one day when he was on the popular CHUM-FM morning show *Roger, Rick and Marilyn*. He diagnosed Marilyn with a bowel problem live on air, which she confirmed.

Things were going well, but major life events were coming for both of us.

A few months after moving downtown, Brough had his friend Paul over and they stayed up having a few beers and talking. Brough fell asleep at around 2:00 a.m. and had a vivid dream.

"It starts off very serene. We're in an old Mustang my father had. My sisters and I are young again, in the back seat. We're driving along the highway. My parents, I can see the backs of their heads. No music, no talking. It's night. You know when you're driving along the highway and the amber highway lights are passing over. The hum of the engine.

"All of a sudden my dad goes, 'What's that?' He looks out the mirror and the police are chasing a car; there's a high-speed chase. It goes right past us. And my parents are like, 'Oh, I want to check that out.' And I said, 'Are you crazy?' So they pull off the highway and we drive into an empty parking lot. My whole family gets out to look around. I'm like, 'Guys, you're crazy. Get back in the car, this is dangerous. Why are you doing this?'"

Brough continued, saying, "The criminal speeds into the parking lot. The cops are nowhere to be seen. He sees our car and says, 'I've got to switch cars.' I'm still in the car and my family's off in the distance now. I try to lock the doors but don't get to the front one quick enough. He opens it, and he has a gun. I say, 'Take the car, I'm too pretty to die,' and I start to run out of the car. He pops me from behind, shoots me. And I don't feel any pain; I fall to my knees, and fall on my back onto the pavement of the parking lot.

"I'm looking at the sky and I've never seen stars so real, and so clear and beautiful. The sky is expanding and I feel myself going into space. And I could feel the cold blood all around me, like a puddle of blood, and it's coming out my mouth. It's scary because if you've ever been at a really high height — I feel like I'm too high, like I'm floating up into the stars. It's terrifying, and I scream, 'No!'

"I wake up and I feel myself dying, without the pain. I look at the clock and it's 4:11. I taste blood, really taste it. So I jump out of bed quick, run to the bathroom, turn on the light, look in the mirror. I'm convinced I'm bleeding. Nothing, no blood. I'm rinsing my mouth out. I'm very disturbed by this dream, my heart is pounding. I go back to bed and finally manage to fall asleep.

"I wake up at 10:00. I see my phone has 57 missed calls and texts since 5:00 a.m. My sister is asking, 'Where are you?' So Aunt Sue, my mom's sister, calls and says, "I'm so sorry, honey, sweetie, your mom's died." And I just fall. I just remember being in a puddle of tears.

"And I just got my suit, got in a cab, and went to my parents' house in Richmond Hill. It's March 10, 2009. I get there, get into the house. Everyone is there."

On the day his mother died, Brough called me, crying, hysterical. I couldn't comprehend what had happened. I wasn't familiar with people just disappearing. I booked the next day off work and drove up to his parents' house to see him. The service was to be right away. "I called *you* first, which was weird because we weren't super close at the time," Brough remembers. "I had other friends that were closer. Something made me rearrange exactly who was important in life."

His parents had been on vacation in the Bahamas. They were on the way to the airport to return home when his mother, Rebecca, decided to stop at a gift shop to pick up some things for the kids. She slipped when stepping off a curb and broke her foot. While healing from the surgery in Toronto, she died of an embolism — a blood clot in the artery.

"At the service I overhear my uncle saying he woke up the night before at 4:05. I say, 'Wait a minute, I woke up at 4:11 from a nightmare.' And he says, 'Well, your mother died at 4:11.' In that moment the room starts spinning, and everything makes me realize that the dream was her spirit reaching out to me. And I was experiencing death *with* her. And keep in mind, my sisters are there for her, and I'm the only one who isn't there. And all those miles away, my spirit and my mother's spirit reach out together. It's very touching in some sense. I've never had an experience like that before or since."

Teenage Brough and his mother, Rebecca.

After the service I stayed with Brough at his apartment, and we sat and talked. At one point, exactly when we mentioned his mother, the kitchen light suddenly went from dim to bright. It was on a dimmer switch and it would seem that the dimmer moved. It wasn't just lights flickering as they sometimes do — the light clearly transitioned from dim to bright as I faced in the direction of the kitchen.

I slept over that night, but the next day I had to get back to my family and job. Brough remembered returning to life and reality in the city too soon, without understanding that he had been traumatized: "My doctor diagnosed me with PTSD and sent me to cognitive behavioural therapy. There was an episode where I had a full-blown anxiety attack and I thought it was a heart attack. And they thought it was a heart attack too, at the hospital. They wheeled me into the resuscitation room, then they recognized it was anxiety and gave me a sedative."

The panic attacks continued and Brough saw the cognitive behavioural therapist. "The philosophy is that how you think creates how you feel. Not how you feel creates how you think. When you have these anxiety attacks you have to ask yourself a series of questions, like 'What have I been thinking about in the last six hours? What have I eaten?' Because you don't normally connect these disparate facts. It's reprogramming your thoughts."

Brough struggled emotionally over the next few years, but he continued his work as a professional medium with a solid base of clients. He spent less time on media appearances and focused on his craft, fine-tuning his ability to deliver information and counselling to people over thousands of sessions, in person and on the phone.

At the same time, I was advancing at work and learning to be a parent. I sporadically experimented with ITC work. I found myself inspired to develop metaphysical and spiritual concepts, stimulated by the work of thinkers like biologist Rupert Sheldrake and physicist David Bohm, who took an open-minded and holistic approach to science. I filled several notebooks with notes and diagrams. I wrote an article for *Reality Sandwich* called "Time Forms," which explored the concept of time having form in the way that physical objects do. The *Reality Sandwich* editors started a book series and asked me if I'd like to write one. The problem I ran into was that as I tried to solidify ideas for a book, I would get on a new path and restructure everything. It wasn't time to write a book quite yet.

Brough and I started to talk about new ideas and projects. We wanted an outlet where we could use humour and talk about concepts related to the paranormal. We decided on a podcast because it would allow us the freedom to act any way we wanted to and cover any subject matter. We found a service that would allow us to broadcast live and take callers, and we had some of our contacts come on as guests. Brough and I would broadcast separately from our own homes and people would call in. We called it *The Psychic Variety Show*, thinking of old variety shows that would mix music, comedy skits, and other acts. The episodes had a frenetic energy and were an experimental but short-lived art form, and we called it off after a couple months and didn't speak for a while.

Despite this being a fertile creative period, there were other fault lines in my life that would shift and cause a quake, turning everything over. Carmen and I had been going to marriage counselling, and while we cared deeply for each other, we were finding it hard to be partners. We made the decision to separate at the start of 2015. I moved out and rented a house close by. Our two girls split their time between the houses. It was the middle of winter and I entered a deep despair for which I was unprepared. In addition to the isolation, I felt self-loathing for disrupting our children's lives and sense of security. Still, they adapted, and Carmen and I stayed cooperative and supportive of each other.

Brough and I started to reconnect around a month after I moved out. Before this, we hadn't had extended periods of time to spend together. Now, I would take the bus to his apartment and we would have some drinks and sometimes I'd sleep on his couch. Brough had recently moved to the same area where I had lived until I was two years old, before moving to Oakville. The house we had lived in was a few blocks away, and at the end of Brough's street was the Church of the Transfiguration, which was attended by my father and my grandparents many years ago.

The boys do a faceswap.

On top of everything else, things were getting rocky at work. The volume of work was slowing down, and I was not seeing eye to eye with one of my peers who had been promoted above me. I knew there was the possibility of being let go. I also knew this could be dangerous for me, emotionally and otherwise, to suffer a job loss so close to my separation. I told a couple of the senior people at work about my situation.

One day I walked into work and up to the third-floor office. I heard a crash and looked out the window. A car had run onto the sidewalk and hit a No Parking sign, causing it to bend over like an axe onto the sidewalk where I had just been. I took note of this, never being one to see things as random. The following week I was let go with severance pay after nine years on the job.

On one hand I felt the excitement of having a chunk of money and the summer to not be tied to any structure. I experienced a sensation of light emitting from my face, as if photons were being released from my skin.

On the other hand, I was in free fall. The feeling of betrayal and the removal of my known structures began to take a toll on me almost right away. I became intermittently paralyzed by despair. At times I was unable to even pick up the phone to call someone for help. It would hit me in debilitating waves. I became aware that we all had in our lives a fabric that maintained our happiness, and often we were not conscious of this fabric. Mine had been damaged badly, which made me conscious of it. I realized that all of the connections I had with people were what sustained my life. Family, friends, acquaintances, co-workers, pets, the person working at the corner store — these were the only real things. I had a new appreciation for those in my life that were still there. I had left behind many friends over the years.

Brough had a new partner, Charles, who also worked as a psychic. Thankfully they weren't far away so I could see them any time. I spent more time with them and they helped to keep me afloat. As always, Brough and I had a hundred ideas floating around for projects we wanted to do together. We talked about doing television shows or another podcast. He got new video equipment and we did a lot of filming. We organized a Meetup group and a bunch of people ended up in my living room one day. We talked about people's experiences with the spiritual and paranormal. It was apparent that people wanted a place to share experiences and connect about this side of their lives.

As we spent more time together, Brough told me about something he had been experiencing over the previous few months. Before he and I reconnected and before he met Charles, he had a period of spending more time alone, and it became a very spiritual time for him. In the mornings as he was waking up, he started to hear a voice speaking. He described it as sounding very wise, and it spoke of universal topics. He couldn't recall the information it had given him, only the feeling that it was a new voice, distinct from what he experienced when giving psychic readings.

This seemed very important to me. After he brought it up a couple times, I suggested we try having a focused session to see if he could encourage this voice to come back and then translate in some way what it was saying. Brough got on board with this idea, and we decided to try it.

I'm Aware of a Presence

We met at Brough's apartment on October 10, Thanksgiving Day, with the intention of getting in touch with the voice that Brough was hearing. We spent a relaxed day together before going out for dinner at The Granite, our usual spot. After dinner we got settled in the living room.

Brough lay on the couch while I sat on the chair beside him. The cats, Monkey and Moo, took turns perching on Brough. I set up my portable audio recorder on the coffee table. We had the door to his balcony open. From nearby, we could hear an ambient buzzing sound, possibly chainsaws. We decided to go ahead, and I turned on the tape recorder.

What follows is a transcript of this first experiment.

BROUGH: Is that sucker [*the audio recorder*] gonna get me from over there?

JOHN: Oh yeah. It'll get everything. But I can move it closer.

BROUGH: Those chainsaws.

JOHN: A lot of lumberjacking going on around.

BROUGH: They're deforesting the city.

[*Long pause, noise continues. We are both quiet, trying to clear our minds.*]

BROUGH: My mind is more chaotic than usual. It's hard to focus. Why is that?

I'm hearing something. See I got, "You have to focus your mind." That's what I was getting.

[*Long pause.*]

I'm aware of a presence. It's not so much that I think it would talk through me as it is that I feel like I could talk to it right now. And maybe get answers that way.

JOHN: Want to try?

BROUGH: Yeah, like, it has to … it's aware of what we're trying to do and it's gotta decide … it's gotta develop a little bit with me to come through me. But it's there.

It's no different than when I'm tuning in and seeing someone's dead father or something. I can get this. My lens is turned onto it.

JOHN: Do you feel it's that same voice you had during that period?

BROUGH: Yeah, it's that thing. It's not as much an identity as it is an incredibly loving presence. And it's, like, it's concerned for you, it's concerned for me, but not in a worried way, in, like — I almost could make out what it was saying: something about you, for a second, now I forget what it was. It's very faint right now, but it's instructing me to focus on it and focus my mind on it right now. To attune to it.

And I feel it's instructing you to come up with a question.

JOHN: Okay. I was wondering that.

BROUGH: And let it come to you, what the question is. Don't be worried about specificity, or if it's too specific, don't worry. Just come up with something that you're led to ask, even if it's about yourself. 'Cause the idea here is to open dialogue.

It's always with us.

[*Pause. Brough's voice becomes more subdued.*]

Even when we don't think of it or realize. Even when we think we're alone. Especially when we think we're alone. Because you're never really alone. The idea of alone stems from a fundamental belief in separation. How can you be separate when even your thoughts interweave with reality?

With each breath that you take and exhale you're pushing air, causing wind. It's like you can't separate spirit from your *self*. Where you begin and where you end is not clear. In that way you're never really alone.

This is something that we've been guided to do. Channelling and everything. It's not the only thing, and certainly it's a good thing to be focusing on ITC and different things of that nature. But this is complementary.

It's not a distraction, it's not meant to be a distraction. Channelling can be a complementary thing. It's almost silly not to use a medium when you have one right there. And it's almost like we're focusing on the screens and on the radios, forgetting that we have a medium that could assist and add to, not be the focus of.

JOHN: I agree. Yeah.

BROUGH: It sounds strange, but it's telling you that your garden's gonna get bigger next year. Like growing a lot more foods from your garden.

JOHN: Mm-hm. That's good. I was concerned about that.

[*I had made my first proper vegetable garden this year at the house I was renting. I don't remember telling Brough, and he hadn't been to my place since I had started it.*]

BROUGH: Like, carrots and everything, like, a lot more.

Like, it's with us always, like, it's almost like ... it's this kind of way in which, and I don't know if this is a suggestion coming from it or if it's coming from me, it's hard to tell. But it's, like, the intentions are really good, we're on the right track, but we're not organizing ourselves properly.

Like, with the camera in Catherine's home — it shouldn't have been her camera, and if we don't have our own, then don't do ITC at that time. Like, it's gotta stay consistent with our equipment, our thing, and our enthusiasm isn't bad, but we have to be organized.

'Cause what we're doing almost with spirit is the equivalent of taking a microphone up to a stranger in public and ambushing them. I mean it's, like, you've got to know what your agenda is and what you're trying to accomplish and what you want. Get that clear in your minds. And then it's as if we'll be able to ask direct questions and get direct answers.

It's almost very much, like, encouraging — I feel a lot of encouragement from it, to keep listening to our intentions and going with it, but we should have questions written down prior to this, and of course, 'cause I'm the channeller, I can't know what they are.

JOHN: I've thought of some questions if you want to go that route. Or if you want to wait, we can do that a bit later.

BROUGH: I'm not sure. I'm not sure. Yeah well, let's see what happens. Why not.

JOHN: Okay. I wanted to ask who Laron is and who Penelope is and what the presence you're talking to — what is their relationship to Laron and Penelope?

[Penelope is the name we identified with the female voice that was heard several times in my EVP recordings, and who we decided was my spirit guide, as Laron was to Brough.]

BROUGH: Everything. Everything. Its relationship is ... it's not, I don't think it's a specific being.

JOHN: Right. But is what you're doing right now the same as talking to Laron?

BROUGH: No. Penelope…

JOHN: Is Penelope to me what Laron is to you? Or is Penelope more specific to ITC?

BROUGH: It's the same as Laron. They know each other now. Laron has been really involved in bringing us together, and Penelope and her have been collaborative. You can almost think of them as our counterparts in spirit.

I don't know if I should say that … it was a joke, there's a little joke there. It's, like, "our better-looking counterparts."

JOHN: [*Laughs.*] Why not say it?

BROUGH: These life guides are beings that have been with us our entire journey. Our physical journey. There's a symbiotic relationship. While they're not having a physical incarnation, they're meant to be learning from the physical incarnation that we're having. And they're also guiding us and helping us learn spiritual lessons. So it's a dichotomy. It's a symbiotic relationship.

In the primitive era, caveman era, before humans were fully developed, there would be … there would be, almost like there wasn't an organized thing, it was like guides were — guides would have been … ghosts. So like an energy, it's like a spirit that's close to the physical plane still learning from something on the physical plane … and following a human host around.

And over the centuries and millennia it became more organized. The guides became more sophisticated. And there was sort of a plan put into place, where it was understood that the guides are still people still learning from the physical but that the human host is a person also needing the guide. In the beginning it was almost like a co-dependent relationship and it's become more healthy over the centuries. Purpose was given. Organization was given. So it's been an evolutionary thing.

You can almost think of them like a soul family. Almost like a soul sibling.

[*There is a knock on the door. I answer it; it's Charles. We chat for a bit and resume with Charles there.*]

So, where do you want me to start? Repeat what I was saying.

JOHN: You were saying that you were having this vision of cavemen in the past and ghosts.

BROUGH: Yeah — primitive cave-dwelling humans, and you know, when you die, not all of them knew what to … it was very primitive; there wasn't a society with history and all that as we understand it.

So a lot of ghosts and people just sort of lingering near the Earth plane still. And some of these entities were, like, following and attaching themselves to living humans, and it was just this chaotic thing and … almost like a symbiotic relationship, like the ghosts were following them around, and then the higher beings help assist in giving purpose.

And it was almost like I saw that these ethereal beings were assisting humans, primitive humans, in not only developing culture and understanding but history and communication. Communication in and of itself was a highly spirit-aided tool.

And these symbiotic sort of relationships between these astral entities that were still close to the Earth and their human counterparts kind of turned into more of an understood sort of spirit guide–human host relationship. Whereas it started off all discombobulated and weird.

JOHN: Yes. So, as we became more structured, so did it become more structured on the other side. In a sense.

BROUGH: Well, the other side always had levels of structure and other civilizations. But these primitive humans didn't cotton on to those levels yet. They were still very discombobulated.

JOHN: Right. So we were kind of a Wild West or whatever.

BROUGH: Yes — with the help of higher beings, not all from Earth. But Earth, Earth is older, in terms of — spiritually speaking — we're on the edge of the galaxy.

JOHN: Mm-hm?

BROUGH: Things close to the centre ... are older. No, no sorry — younger.

JOHN: Younger? Yeah.

BROUGH: We're older. We're on the edge, we're on the fringe. And then it stopped there. Charlie knocked.

JOHN: Right. Thanks Charlie, we were just about to solve all of human history.

BROUGH: Literally all the mysteries that we struggle with. Literally about to solve them. I finally get the answer, and then you had to knock.

CHARLES: Well, spirit orchestrates all things over time.

BROUGH: Well, spirit, *nyah nyah nyah...*

* * *

Sometime later, Brough and I looked back at this first attempt. We struggled to recall the physical setting of the encounter.

JOHN: I think it was in the evening.

BROUGH: Yeah, I remember it was dark.

JOHN: But I think it was just the usual in the sense that you got into a sedate kind of state, you felt sedate. Your eyes got a bit heavy.

BROUGH: I remember being nervous that I wasn't going to be able to produce anything. And I was afraid of it being contrived and in my own imagination. I was very conscientious of *that*. And I knew how interested in this you were. And I didn't want to let you down. And I think I got more than I vocalized. Because I was, like, "Whoa, I don't know what this is and I don't know if I trust it."

JOHN: Okay, so some things, you weren't confident it wasn't coming from you?

[*I'm asking him if he wasn't sure if it was coming from his own mind, or being channelled.*]

BROUGH: Yup. So that's why this first session is very, let's say, well, far more generalized than our later sessions that were to follow.

JOHN: Do you remember the types of things that you weren't vocalizing?

BROUGH: Probably things that would sound like … that would sound like the intentions of the channelling. Like, "I brought you together" or "We've been together for a long time" or "We intend to continue to do this" or "This is what the project will look like." That's what I vaguely remember, being like, "Whoa, I didn't sign up for no project."

JOHN: Oh, okay. It's stuff that did come through later. But you were a little taken aback, maybe, that they were talking about a project.

BROUGH: Yeah. You know me and any kind of work…

JOHN: Well, that's interesting. Because all we knew was that we were going to try to have this voice talk. We didn't necessarily know this was a project. Although I was all ready to sign up for it.

BROUGH: Yeah. Well, that's part of it! I could sense that you were. And I thought, *Well, am I just reading him? Is this an external voice?* I wanted to make sure it was really external. That was important to me. I remember that. And that's perhaps the only thing that got somewhat in the way.

But it was a pretty strong link, you know? And the thing is, there's a distinction. The voice that I would hear when I was fifteen, and the voice that I heard in my late twenties, the higher self voice that we were just talking about, that's like a direct voice in my head, very loud, talking to me and feeding me mental concepts as well as words.

The readings that I do and channelling that we do are a different channel entirely [*from the inner voice*]. I get imagery with readings and with [*the inner voice*] I see distortions. We get sparkles. I see lights. And you've seen the strange lights, the blue lights, the purple lights. I see that, and sometimes get shapes. And I sort of speak it before I think it, if there's any way to express that. It's just coming out of my mouth.

JOHN: That's an interesting distinction. So you're not getting the thought and then verbalizing it.

BROUGH: Yeah. It's almost using my body, really. Like a medium.

All in Small

It was four months before we made a second attempt at channelling. Prior commitments and the holidays kept us occupied until we were finally able to meet again. We already had an event planned for just after our first session in October, in which we rented out a church, and I gave a multimedia presentation, and Brough did spontaneous readings for people in the crowd. This attracted about 80 people, which was encouraging for future endeavours.

On February 3, 2016, a Wednesday evening, we took our places in Brough's apartment, with him on the couch and me in the chair. Things started to happen within a minute of our getting into position. With this contact, I was able to engage in dialogue with the Voice and speak to them about technology and civilization.

BROUGH: Okay. All right, wow. I feel like I'm already tapped in. I feel like they're like, "Of course," like they were, like, this was a spirit team, and it's like, everything that's been happening today, and they're helping out, and it's like, "Of course, where do you think we are." Or it's almost like their feeling is like, "You don't really think you're doing this on your own, do you?" That's the feeling I get.

Aha. Hold on.

Did you have questions that were geared more to them explaining who they are and talking more about guides and things like that, first?

JOHN: I did originally have that, yes. That was the first idea.

BROUGH: You wanted to get more personal with them.

JOHN: Yeah, and I can do that.

BROUGH: No, you had the right idea to change your mind. Actually — or was it your idea really? You're in communication with them too.

The link hasn't been forged clearly enough yet for a personality to come through and for me to embody yet. It hasn't been developed sufficiently yet. So you were veered off from that question because it's neither the time nor place, it's neither here nor there. We'll get to know them when the time comes, probably when I'm able to go more into full trance.

Let me just see what they want.

It's, like, possible that there'll be a day where I can go into full trance. I'll just be asleep and I won't even be conscious.

JOHN: Oh! Okay.

BROUGH: But yeah, go ahead. You can ask questions and we'll see what happens. They like this format; it's not necessarily the only format we'll use, but this is an interesting one.

JOHN: Yeah. Okay. So, the topics I was thinking of for tonight were to do with some things I've been reading. I've been reading a book by Graham Hancock, and I went to see a lecture by him. He's basically about looking at ancient civilizations from before the Ice Age.

BROUGH: Well, you know there's a reason why I was listening to Graham Hancock on Art Bell all morning.

JOHN: Today?

BROUGH: Yes, today. I can show you the history on my iPad.

JOHN: I believe it. Oh, wow that's interesting.

BROUGH: I had never heard of Graham Hancock before. And I was guided to that randomly. "Randomly." [*Brough uses air quotes here.*]

JOHN: Oh, oh, isn't that neat. Okay. 'Cause one of the women that was at our event, Kaye, had sent me an invite to his lecture at Bloor Cinema, like, a month ago.

BROUGH: Wow, that recent.

JOHN: Yeah, and I read his book before that, which was called *Magicians of the Gods*. So he's looking at ancient sites, and there's one in Turkey that was recently unearthed that's about ten or eleven thousand years old, minimum. He's putting together clues and the idea is that there've been cycles in the past, there've been civilizations before our currently recognized one.

BROUGH: Which is true.

JOHN: And what I'm interested to talk about is cycles of our civilization in the past. Do we go through cycles where we develop, and then we start over again? Why does this happen? Is there some kind of cataclysmic process, like meteorites, earthquakes, and so on, that make a civilization start over? And why is it that they have to start over, and are we on a path towards something like that? That would be my first topic.

[*At this point in the conversation, it occurs to me that Brough is no longer speaking as himself. While there is no clear-cut way for me to determine when this transition was made, it's based on his speech becoming slower and more deliberate, and on the communication taking on a greater depth. In subsequent sessions, I will change the speaker name from BROUGH to VOICE when this transition is made. We'll see further on that Brough will refer to himself in the second person, making it clear that he is not speaking as Brough.*]

VOICE: Yeah, very good.

Well, what humanity hasn't discovered yet or isn't ready to understand yet is that everything is blueprinted. Right down to the subatomic and even beyond. And that so-called inventions are more like remembering what's already true. Instead of "invention," you can think of it as a "remembrance."

And earlier versions of humanity were heading in the direction that we are now, and sometimes a cataclysm would get in the way, sometimes a plague, sometimes a war, sometimes, well you could either look at it from a situational, almost a circumstantial problem, which would be like an asteroid coming from outside, or you could look at it as an internal problem, where people are conflicted inside to tear the society apart.

And the reason why those primitive civilizations didn't form technologies and certain inventions that we have today, modern inventions that we take for granted, was because at that time they were more primitive. Try to remember that the brain and the body, the human body, is evolving over time. So it becomes more capable as time goes on.

It would be ideal if it could just start from the beginning and just continue uninterrupted, but sometimes these interruptions do happen. But life will continue and what is meant to be will be fulfilled.

JOHN: And the interruption, I see it as a synchronistic type of event: If a meteor hits, for example, I don't see it as ever being a random event.

VOICE: Well, nothing is random. What we call randomness is simply a pattern too large to see.

JOHN: Right. So then I would think that there must be some type of cause for it to happen at that particular time. Something as major as a meteor that would end a civilization and a good portion of life on the Earth. There must be factors that go into the timing of that.

VOICE: Usually for patterns at that level, patterns that are happening at such a large level, the timing was decided long before the civilization even existed. But this gets into the nature of mind, you see, because on that level, if you imagine the meteor itself, if you imagine every facet of the universe as being at one with itself, then indeed a species, indeed each individual of that species, as a collective whole, would agree to so-called end itself in its current form, to cause a restart or a resetting effect, if you will. That was all decided before anyone even got here. That was decided at ethereal levels of existence.

Going back to the blueprint concept, you could almost imagine your physical universe as being loosely strung onto the hanger of spirit. The skeletal structure or the framework of the universe could be considered the astral realms or the spiritual realms as you were. Almost like most of the universe is made up of dark matter, which really is just a word for the undetectable.

So these events are not isolated and random as much as they're part of a larger fabric of existence, a larger script.

JOHN: If the entire thing is an organism, then the meteor is just one part of the organism.

VOICE: Precisely.

But it should be stated that there won't be a meteor collision for quite some time, and by the time that you're due for a large one, you'll likely have the technology to avert it.

JOHN: That's interesting. And that's part of our development? To be able to develop to the point of having the technology where we can ensure that we can continue?

VOICE: That's right. In the twenty-third century, when there would have been a disastrous meteor, you'll already have mining facilities and thruster controls on most of these dangerous rocks. You'll even be able to literally smash them into each other.

JOHN: Mm-hm. It's interesting because one contradiction I felt in Graham Hancock's talk was him saying that we've reached this level where everything's terrible and we're so technology-focused and so on and away from nature and destroying the planet, but he's also saying that we can get it together and prevent one of these meteors, but that's only possible because of the technology. So it's almost a bit — people tend to look at technology as a negative, but on the other hand it's really all how you use it, I suppose, and your attitude towards technology.

VOICE: Ah yes, but the arrogance of man, to think trees are natural but his buildings are not. As the ant hill is considered part of nature, technology and space travel and computers and buildings and everything that you take for granted in your modern world is indeed just another extension of nature and natural law. Indeed, the definition of nature should be extended, that if it operates on principles of natural law then it must be a part of nature.

Anyway, lots of people have negative points of view. In some ways you can say technology can also bring you closer to nature — make you more a part of it and appreciate it more. Such is the case with devices you could use to clean the atmosphere, clean your water as well, assist in the growth of trees and restoration of forests. Technology can be your greatest saving grace as well as your greatest enemy.

JOHN: Yes. And technology has really been with us since the beginning of being human.

VOICE: Ah, it brings up an interesting question, doesn't it — it's not what it is, it's what you use it for.

I think that Graham Hancock has the right idea in the sense that humanity has become disconnected with itself, and indeed if it were to connect with the things that are important, it maybe indeed would start to use its own technology and use its own abilities to enhance nature and help nature and heal versus destroy.

JOHN: And work together to organize itself to address the possibility of meteors, I suppose.

VOICE: Yes, which actually should be a primary focus at this point in humanity. The threat of asteroids and solar storms is perhaps a more important task than sending young people to war.

JOHN: On the other hand, part of me also thinks that, with being part of nature, being part of the larger system that we're part of, isn't it a bit like overdoing it with antibiotics? If we focus on these threats, as they're seen, which are also part of nature, and if nature decides that we should have a meteor come our way, should we stop it?

VOICE: Hm. Yes of course, a sandwich could feed you and sustain you and keep you alive, but you could also choke to death on it. Who's to say, in that point of view, that these asteroids aren't valuable sources of minerals, so that you wouldn't destroy your planet.

After all, they are remnants and leftovers of raw materials given off by a star in the creation of planets; so rather than destroying a fragile — already fragile — and delicately balanced ecosystem, wouldn't it make sense that the asteroids were a source of plenty for any kind of advanced culture to eventually tap into rather than tampering with the delicate balance of the ecosystems on their planet?

One could say that asteroid mining is a natural step for any species that becomes spacefaring.

JOHN: Asteroid mining. Yes. Okay. Interesting.

VOICE: Brings up the saying "Ripe for the taking." They also said the same thing about electricity, along the lines of what your discussion is about. Man could use electricity to cook his meal, or electricity could cook a man.

JOHN: *Ha ha!* Yeah. And Thomas Edison used to electrocute dogs in front of crowds to demonstrate how dangerous electricity was.

VOICE: Yes, he'd do anything to put down Tesla.

And Tesla, in very similar demonstrations, which came first, was demonstrating how tech — how electricity — could raise the hair on his head and cause great benefit to the world. Of course, Tesla was right.

Edison wanted to demonstrate the destructive powers of it. So in any argument, you can see the good and the bad, but one of the gifts of humanity is to focus on the good, and what you focus on with your consciousness causes it to grow — this is a concept that many are starting to understand but few put into practice.

In fact — correction — many put into practice; they often expect the worst and get exactly what they wished for. Often at great detriment to themselves.

JOHN: Now, we've had such a rapid growth in technology, obviously, just even in our lifetimes, we see communication systems developing at an incredible rate. I find for me, personally, I make an effort to use them in a measured way — phones and so on — and have it in my life to the point where it's useful but it doesn't preoccupy me.

So I think that's probably part of what people, each person, has to develop, is a sense of how technology can be in their lives in a healthy way, and they can still maintain their natural psychological states without constantly being preoccupied with it.

VOICE: Yes, John, you're way ahead of your time. This is a truth, that with many new things, as with a child that first gets their hand on candy, they go overboard until they make themselves sick. But of course, in line with the conversation, technology can be a great thing if you use it wisely, with wisdom and with spiritual guidance. And it sounds to me like you're doing just that.

JOHN: Trying to.

I wanted to talk a little more about phases of civilization, of human civilization. Even within our own recorded history, we have phases; we have the Information Age, we have the Industrial Age and the Bronze Age and the Iron Age and so on.

But then there's this larger idea that in some religions of larger cycles of time, like the Mayans have, I think Hindu religion has cycles of time spanning thousands, hundreds of thousands of years, and I think the idea is also with astrological cycles, that there are different astrological periods that have different characteristics related to the different signs, like Pisces or what have you.

And I was wondering about that — if there are different periods that we go through that have different sorts of characteristics, maybe in our environment, in our psyche, that are sort of different conditions for us to live in and develop in.

VOICE: Yes, well, isn't it interesting that pyramids were being built at all corners of the Earth, even when the builders had no way of communicating with each other, or so it seemed. As we said earlier, what you call invention is often just remembrance, or in other words, a natural unfolding of the design that was already within you. What goes on *without* is as *within*. You might as well replace the word "matter" with "mirror."

There do appear to be ages, as there seem to be in the physical world. A beginning, a middle, and an end. But due to the laws of eternity and the nature of the undying self, what begins has a middle, and ends and begins again. This is a universal truth that we understand on our side that you do not yet understand on yours. You who still believe in a finite existence and have no way of understanding the nature of eternity.

One day, instead of seeing things as a constantly flowing river, you'll look at life itself as a spiral. Always made of the same thing, expanding, expanding, and expanding as it circles and orbits in on the original core principle. Many layers, like the layers of an onion. Everything in your nature is a symbol of reality at a higher level. The word "all" is in the word "small."

And that's perhaps the best way to think about it for the time being. Whereas in the spirit world, or in the astral realms, there are many concepts that are fully developed, many advanced levels that you'll only appear to be able to see and interact with as you yourself become more advanced and aware and able to accept your inner being at deeper levels.

But would you believe it if it was stated that everything that ever will be already is and already was? It's just a process of unfolding, like a flower blooming. Or a baby developing into a small child, into a young adult. The blueprint was always there.

While you experience three-dimensional space and the fourth dimension of time, as you understand it in this current form, everything appears to be nothing until it's something. Whereas the whole idea should be that when you're growing, you're really only becoming yourself. Perhaps then parents wouldn't feel the need so much to force their children other than encourage their natural abilities. A common mistake people make with themselves, which they've learned from their parents, is to think that they're like a piece of clay that needs to be moulded and shaped.

One of your great artists used to say that there was a person waiting in the piece of marble; he just needed to find it.

Does this concept make sense to your question?

JOHN: It makes a lot of sense, but I'm trying to actually remember what my question was.

VOICE: You were asking about the cycles.

But it does kind of defeat the question in the sense that cycles are a byproduct of the pattern of remembering self. And it appears right now that humanity is making great leaps and great advances in a short time. This is because, for the first time in history, it is allowed to. It does not actually have to worry as much about its own survival. It's well fed, and it has the freedom to think about higher pursuits.

JOHN: Okay. That's interesting. So, you'd say that that is the first time in the history of humanity that that's happened?

VOICE: It's happened in very small groups before, but never at this level. Never to this capacity.

JOHN: So in the past, you'd have more isolated civilizations developing technology, but not in the global worldwide way that it's being done now?

VOICE: Of course. And then, those isolated ones were often the ones with the most money, the most resources. They were well fed and had the freedom to start to develop and focus on higher pursuits. And the neighbouring tribes that were stuck in destitution would often come knocking with pitchfork and flame in hand. To rob the richer ones of their resources.

Only when an equilibrium occurred, due to inspired ideas and good leadership, for a short time, did we start to have equilibrium in society, for everyone to begin to think of "all" as part of one whole and to begin the unification process.

JOHN: The unification process.

VOICE: It's what you would call modern society, civilized man. Where we for the most part focus less on killing each other and more on creating sustainability and a sense of global community.

JOHN: And are we headed in that direction?

VOICE: Oh, compared to where it used to be, we're already there. But there are still primal instincts and there are still people with regressionist agendas and regressionist ideas who resist progress and resist technology and cling to superstition.

JOHN: But what about, say, Aboriginal peoples of North America or of Australia, who did not develop in the technological sense that we have? Of course, they had technology, but would they be considered superstitious or primitive?

VOICE: Oh, not at all. Not at all. They represent an aspect of humanity that has forgotten itself. And thusly they have been forgotten. They had such balance with nature that they did really not need much to do with technology. They were well fed and in perfect harmony with nature.

JOHN: So why do we need technology then?

VOICE: Technology's not so much a need as it is risen from creativity and the developed mind; it's a part of nature. Not every species is designed to travel through space, but humanity, like many other humanoid species, is designed for space travel. Technology, in the form that you mean, is almost always geared toward reaching the stars.

JOHN: So, is technology really, at its heart, a form of creativity then?

VOICE: Oh yes, a byproduct of creativity, to be sure.

JOHN: As opposed to necessity.

VOICE: A mixture of both. It's creativity that meets necessity.

JOHN: Necessity as the mother of invention.

VOICE: Mm. But when you need not so much anymore and you have a chance to stick to your grassroots, as it were, and you are well fed and you want for nothing, the mind begins to grow. And sometimes in some ways becomes bored and looks for new ways to entertain itself. New ways to expand, new ways to enhance and endure and create life. Technology in some ways is the birth child to humanity.

There will come a day where technology won't be needed as much anymore, at least not in any form that you would recognize. Because the powers of the mind are vast. It is possible to move through the universe, and even in some ways, evolve past the need of a physical form, without death itself. But technology is a stepping stone. An antenna, as it were.

JOHN: Is it a way of developing our minds? Because we make this thing external, this idea, and that's the first step, the invention of it. But then the next step is to learn how to organize it and control it and use it responsibly once it's been created.

VOICE: Yes, but then what of the days when the final step is to merge with it again, until it is a part of you? Then it is not an external thing at all.

JOHN: And does that mean making the technology disappear altogether? Because we've developed those capabilities within our minds?

VOICE: Well, it would appear to disappear. But what came out of you eventually comes back in. Part of the cycle. There was a time when gigantic snails existed, and birds that you now call seagulls were able to easily eat them. And when those snails became extinct or went away, the seagulls eventually learned how to pick up mussels and clam shells and smash them on the rocks by flying high and dropping them above rocks. And in a sense, this is a technology; the seagull uses the rock as a technology to open the clam.

It's really no different. There are certain things that are more a necessity. But the kind of technology we're talking about is not primitive stone and bear skins. The technology we're discussing is technology humanity has used to extend itself. To reach further than its own limitations allowed before. And indeed, that's a symbol of the day that will come eventually, in many millennia, when humanity itself will disappear as you know it and become a higher form of life altogether.

Much like the clam must be smashed against the rock in order for the bird to get to the goods, if you think of space as a challenge, humanity will throw itself against the greatest challenges in order to test its limits and then further learn to extend itself.

JOHN: Mm-hm.

Still, there's the prevailing materialist view within science, within technology, which holds that the idea of consciousness over matter, and telepathy and so on, is superstition. I see that needing to change, and perhaps it already is changing. But I can see the role of telepathy or psychic ability coming more into the mainstream instead of things being purely focused on technology, so there could be maybe some combination of the two happening. In a recognized, open way.

VOICE: Well, that's exactly true; it will take time. But that's part of the natural progression.

JOHN: And then that would surely affect the way we develop technology, if the mind is then incorporated into technology as a real causative factor.

VOICE: Technology will cradle the mind. With the invention of quantum computers, which are already well in the making, there will be a form of artificial intelligence, which will eventually be able to bolster and simulate human intelligence and human consciousness, as you were. Indeed, spirits and souls can even move through them and use them.

And then in millennia from then, humanity will be able to merge its consciousness with its machines, and its machines with its consciousness.

Machines won't even have a metallic structure, as you would understand it. A lot of them will start to be crystalline in nature. A lot of them will operate on principles of zero-point energy and be in total harmony and rhythm with the universe. Then people will be able to think themselves from one place to another quite easily. Much like you've heard we can do in the astral realm, which is true.

Which is where, as I said, all invention exists, for you as you create it and appear to think it up, it's really just a remembrance of what already always was and always will be.

JOHN: There's this idea of pan-psychism in philosophy which says that everything is conscious and has a consciousness, from atoms up to trees, to rocks, even, well, anything. And that makes sense to me, that everything has a consciousness, and one idea I have been exploring a bit is the idea that even machines are conscious — that any object is conscious according to the nature of the object itself.

So an atom has an atomic consciousness, and then a molecule that the atom is a part of has a greater consciousness, in the same way that, say, the human is conscious and also each part of our body is conscious. But then I'm also thinking that a machine could develop its own consciousness, like a car or a computer could be inhabited by a form of consciousness, determined by the purpose of that machine — that the car takes on a type of a car consciousness and is aware of its purpose as a car.

VOICE: Hm. A fish is the ocean, and the ocean is the fish. You think of the consciousness as a field, and all objects in your world as being within that field, extensions of that field, and yes of course, everything is consciousness. That is true. The world is an extension of thought.

JOHN: And that would extend even to things that have been created by humans, not just objects in the natural world. And they would take on their own awareness — so in that way, we are endowing consciousness to something. Or at least creating a container for the field of consciousness to enter into.

VOICE: Exactly. It is not your intention with your devices, you entering consciousness into them. To give purpose to something. Much like many feel that God or a great spirit has given them a personal deed or personal purpose.

Indeed, the more we ponder this, the more it begs the question of personal responsibility, spiritual responsibility. Your children and the things you create require love to guide them — spirit, wisdom.

Humanity, in many ways, is so out of touch it is allowing cruelty and ego to take charge of its decisions. Talking about the use of consciousness and machinery, right now, in Russia, innocent animals, monkeys, are being sent into space in cruel experiments performed on them. Unable to process what's happening to them, experiencing sheer terror, often losing consciousness and passing out at the sheer shock of it all. And humanity loves to tell itself that these creatures have no consciousness.

It's a big enough stretch for people to accept that inanimate matter is still a byproduct of consciousness. To imagine telling these people that these innocent monkeys have consciousness and for them to shrug that off — it goes to show man's inherent nature when it comes to wanting to separate himself from nature itself.

One thinks that when man came up with a bible that said God created man in his image, man took it too literally. Man thinks it is a god and forgets that it is a part of nature, a part of the whole. And if man forgets that, then man forgets who he is and instead lives in a delusional state of mind.

[*Authors' note: We are aware that some ideas here are conveyed using male-centered language. Rather than change it after the fact, we would like to make this a topic for a future discussion. Also, there are other discussions in this book that provide insight into the Voice's point of view on sex and gender, and it is not male-centered.*]

JOHN: And yet, we do have this *ability* to separate ourselves from nature, so clearly we were given this ability for a reason. But I suppose it's our duty to become aware of that difference in ourselves.

VOICE: Man has many abilities. But it was never written that man would never make a mistake. The more abilities that you have, the more chances of something going wrong.

Separation wasn't so much an idea given to man as it was his way of understanding why "here" and "over there" appears to be true. But by the same token, paranormal phenomena, as you'd call it — synchronicity, psychic phenomena — all point toward oneness. And are reminders for man to resist the temptation to separate himself from his other.

JOHN: Why did people develop from nature? Is it simply a development of nature?

VOICE: You're forgetting that people existed before this planet even existed. That there was a cosmic blueprint. And your soul, as it were, decided to create the planet, to create conditions for life. And to create those conditions so specifically that the exact kind of life that it wanted would then form.

Everything is predetermined at a level much higher than you would understand.

JOHN: So rather than people developing out of nature—

VOICE: People developed nature as a form of technology to develop. Indeed, the body is a form of technology. Who you are is not the body. Which is not to confuse with the separation idea, because the body is an extension of your thought.

JOHN: Yes. And you mentioned synchronicity, and that's how I have been feeling about synchronicity recently, is that it's kind of a completion of a circuit, in which nature, our environment, is communicating information to us. And so, the source is then communicating with the product, I guess.

VOICE: Yes. Again, patterns at levels much higher than you can see with your limited scope becoming revealed to you.

JOHN: [*Sensing Brough beginning to tire.*] How do you feel?

BROUGH: [*Groans.*] I feel it fading a bit. But they're making me feel like it's okay, it doesn't matter, we'll just do it again later.

JOHN: Do you want to call that one a night?

BROUGH: Yeah. I like that. I feel like they were in charge. I feel like they were helping with everything that happened today for me.

JOHN: Yeah, I feel that way too.

BROUGH: And now I feel even better about it because I feel like it's part of the bigger thing. Was that all right?

JOHN: That was amazing. I can hardly wait to write it down.

Growth and Evolution

Whatever was happening, we started to feel like we could get it to happen on a regular basis, and we got into a regular rhythm of sessions, or least attempts at them. We would end up having days when nothing was coming through, and there was some trial and error in figuring out the conditions that allowed channelling to happen and in realizing that it wasn't always under our control whether or not it would happen at all.

We always met at his apartment, and I never proposed that we try channelling at my place. I think it was important to hold the sessions where Brough felt comfortable and at ease, which meant his own environment, with his cats nearby. Brough had had a few apartments in the city, and this was his nicest one, in a clean modern building uptown, on the ninth floor, with a panoramic view of Lake Ontario.

Usually I would take the subway up there after work, and either we would have a session that night or I would crash on the couch and we would try in the morning after breakfast. Mornings were generally good because we were refreshed and in tune with each other after spending some time together. If we tried in the evening, I noticed that things went better if we went out for a walk or for dinner first and hung out and talked for a while. We had to open up the channel between the two of us before looking outward.

On February 16, our third session, I slept over on the couch. I was woken up at around 6:00 a.m. by the sound of something bumping on the floor behind me, and three rapid claps. There was nothing there. Brough got up and made us breakfast. He liked to cook and usually made me giant portions of food while I sat on the couch.

I started the recorder and we went into our usual positions — him lying on the couch, me in the comfy chair. Most sessions start with us just talking. This session began with us discussing the sounds that woke me up so early in the morning. From there, our voices delivered some longer, more in-depth monologues on the topic of evolution and growth, and we in turn could feel the evolution and growth of our unusual project.

BROUGH: So, you heard clapping that woke you up?

JOHN: Yep. Sleeping on the couch here. Around six, I heard the sound of something falling on the floor behind me, some kind of *bump*. But I couldn't see anything on the floor that had fallen. It was like a *bump* and then *clap-clap-clap*, very quickly. Which woke me right up.

BROUGH: Okay, so, I'm hoping that was a spirit encounter. We're hoping that means we'll have some energies with us to assist in the channelling attempt number three. [*In nerd voice:*] *Number three point oh.* All right. I shall assume the position. That's what they said: "Assume the position."

JOHN: You have a position?

BROUGH: My position is fetal. I already look like a big baby.

[*I start laughing and get the giggles.*]

BROUGH: I wonder if they haven't figured out what they wanna say.

JOHN: Do they have to figure things like that out? I think they would just sort of *know*.

BROUGH: I guess. I think sometimes it's a process of involving thought transference, so they have to kinda have some kind of loose script as to know what to transfer. There's a little bit of a process.

JOHN: Right. I think we just need to give it a little time to ... hook up.

BROUGH: I need my sunglasses for this nonsense. The sun is shining in the window.

[*We talk for a while, mainly comedy, about how channellers are stuck in the Ron Burgundy era with wood-panelled basements and glasses of scotch. After a while we go quiet and there is a long pause before Brough starts again.*]

BROUGH: All right, something's happening ... I can feel a shift, like they're assisting and raising my vibrations here. Like a lightness to my mood. It's funny, they must be on a frequency that's not common for humans, 'cause I didn't feel particularly down to begin with; I feel pretty good, but this is, like, really nice, this is lovely. This is like a feeling of lightness and no cares, no worries, I guess 'cause I've had some ongoing worries lately that you get used to having and then you don't realize they're there. But now I'm above that. That's a nice treat.

I think I heard, just now, I thought I heard, "Yes, there are many things, many worries you hold on to that we do not possess. A lot which concerns you does not concern us. Of course, that is the nature of being in the physical world. We bring you greetings. You're allowed to interact with us."

I think that means say hello, JT.

[*Brough sometimes calls me JT, which he picked up from Natasha, who connected us.*]

JOHN: Hi. Greetings to you as well.

BROUGH: One moment ... they're still trying to attune me to something here. The noise that you heard was a woman. I'm getting the word "Alice" or a name similar to this.

JOHN: Okay.

BROUGH: She's what they would call a "principal communicator." It's not quite Alice. They'll give it to me correctly later. But it's along those lines, it's an A-L sound to me. They're part of the group that brought us together in the beginning. The synchronicities, the 22s. They were working to encourage and to form a team. On this side of the world, on this side of the dimensional ... thing. I think they just said, "on this side" and then I'm trying to add.

They wanted to form something for communication purposes. With the potential of development. They require good receivers. So they found a psychic and they look for other personalities that are receptive individuals with their own psychic talents. There was to be a third but they had some trouble getting that one to pay attention. It's not Anita. They may still be able to bring them to us.

JOHN: We don't know this person?

BROUGH: No, not yet.

Had they been able to listen and fall in line to some degree, I think that our development process would have been shorter. But now it's sufficient where we can communicate and we were able to do it just the two of us. They're saying, "As you would say, some things do not always go according to plan." They've got a bit of humour to them. It's not as dry as I'm making it sound.

JOHN: This person is male or female?

BROUGH: Female.

JOHN: That's what I thought.

BROUGH: She's very stubborn. It would have been a very different dynamic than what we're used to. In many ways she would have represented the matriarch. Kept us in line.

JOHN: Hm!

BROUGH: Our mutual respect for her would have forced us to sort of … capitulate. In the process of looking for receptors, they also consider personality and interplay dynamics. When creating groups like this.

JOHN: I've found with musical groups there seems to be a kind of perfect formation of people in terms of their talents and personalities. Is that something that's been used to form musical groups before?

VOICE: The principles are the same. With musical groups, most musical groups are formed based on the individuals who become part of the group. The only difference is that this, what we're talking about now, is governed by spirit. In a sense they already are the band and they're just looking for the instruments now. To extend your analogy, have you noticed that mediums often say "tuning in" or "being tuned"? As you are the instrument, for spirit.

JOHN: Oh, okay. And so, you think you'll continue to try to influence her or communicate with her?

[*Brough's voice deepens and he sounds like he is starting to speak as them. He is lying on the couch sideways, eyes closed, with his hand partly covering his mouth.*]

VOICE: As you may say, anything is possible. But for right now, you have developed sufficiently, over the past ten years, to begin to build a bridge that we had initially intended for. We see you as children, you see. You are precious to us. We have followed you since before you've been even aware of us.

The first theme you'll notice that we cover with you is evolution. But not evolution of the physicality as it were — evolution of the soul, and how it actually ties into the evolution of physicality. You see, as the tail does not wag the dog, spirit is in charge. The physical falls into line, always. For without spirit, there is no physical.

And much as is the case with everything in your world, there need be development. For when you are born into the physical, you begin developing, from the age of an infant, into a young child, into a teenager, into an adult. It seems in nature that everything has a developmental curve.

This principle remains true, even in our side of life. Albeit it appears to happen much, much more slowly. Some would say slowly because things appear to be static here, for the most part. And yet there are realms and beings that represent great advancement, that you can see, almost at will, with a sufficiently developed mind.

The difference that I could compare it to would be as follows: Imagine watching a time-lapse video in your world, of a rose blooming. In my world, we simply have the entire roll of film and you can skip to any frame you wish.

But one of the laws is that you must have a developed mind in order to see a developed world. Much as you feel prisoner to your body many days, a spirit entity could be described as prisoner to its mind. And this is why the emphasis is put on development and growth and evolution.

The further you develop, the more you can see and interact with higher realms. And *that* law stays true, both in your world as much as in ours. Indeed, the two are interconnected. Does this make sense to you?

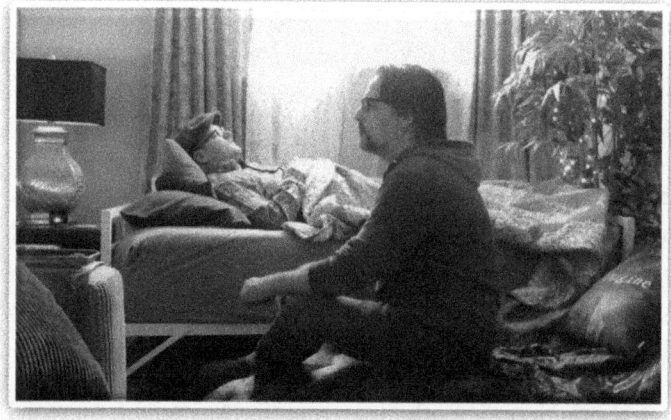

Brough and John in a channelling session.

JOHN: Yes. I'm just extremely happy that this is happening and moving along. It's getting me a bit emotional. I'm just absorbing it.

VOICE: Yes. Well, good work, well done. We too are happy and proud.

JOHN: I feel like this is what we've been building to, and I think without even knowing it, this is what I always wanted to happen.

VOICE: Ah, you did know, but perhaps you mean, *not conscious of*. For just as the rose becomes a rose, it once was a seed. All of the information to become a rose was within it already. It is simply, as I said, a matter of development. A step toward the future.

There are many people who would not like this concept at all. Many people who would like to believe that they're complete and whole and with absolutely no work to do. These people are, of course, in denial of a fundamental truth in nature.

Last time, we referred to the spiral of life. Do you recall?

JOHN: I don't think I remember that.

VOICE: Hm. It is in the recording.

In your minds, many of you hold an idea of evolution as being linear, from start to finish. Almost as you'd call a bell curve, on a graph. Whereas evolution is actually a spiral, leading out from a centre.

In many ways, as you evolve, you can look within and see every step, every process, every level. And the more you seem to change, the more you stay the same. Just simply with expanded ideas. Growth in every direction.

The question is, what has inspired you to grow? What is the driving force? It is not biology you see. It is spirit. The will, the desire, to know itself, to expand itself, to reach out in every direction and connect. But the concept of separation, albeit apparently a true experience, is a foreign one to spirit. For spirit seeks to connect.

Where a bond has been broken, spirit works tirelessly to heal and make whole. When you have been forgotten, spirit remembers.

Where gaps and distances, vast oceans that seem insurmountable appear to exist, spirit will cross it and build a bridge for others to follow.

The great duality of the universe and all of its dimensions appear to show that separation, disconnection, darkness are a constant. And on the opposite end, spirit continuously works to heal and make whole. It was once said that peace is stronger than war because peace heals. Is this not true?

So you see, this is what we endeavour to do. This is your sole purpose. And your *soul* purpose.

As agents of healing, ambassadors of spirit, your job is and will always be to help people find a way: Where they are hopeless, to bring hope. But always remember, you do not do this alone. For to do it alone would infer, again, separation. And we are never far.

The term "love" as you understand it is an insufficient word for this moment. As we have a deep and unending care for you.

You are not alone.

[*Long pause.*]

BROUGH: That's it. There's no more.

[*Pause.*]

JOHN: I got very teary.

BROUGH: Oh, you got a little emotional?

JOHN: Yes.

BROUGH: I can hear this but I don't necessarily take it in. I'm doing it through the same thing that I do readings every day.

JOHN: I can see that it's coming through you, you're channelling.

BROUGH: Yeah. 'Cause I don't remember it per se, and I don't have any agenda in my head. I'm just the speaker.

JOHN: I wonder if they stopped because I was getting emotional … or, I wasn't sure.

BROUGH: No. No, they have a plan. And they're going to tell us more next time but they don't want to do too much too fast. And they're aware that we have things to do today. But it's very beautiful. I thought that was really nice.

JOHN: I just became overwhelmed, just feeling that this was really happening and, like, this is what I've always wanted to do and wanted us to do. And also feeling proud of you.

BROUGH: Oh, thanks, JT.

JOHN: I really, really was. Just the way they were talking, I could feel that it was something else coming through. It's beautifully written, it's just beautifully worded.

And it's funny because I realized that I don't remember a lot of it at the time, because there's so much, it's so densely packed with concepts. And they're saying, "Do you remember this thing from last time?" and I was like, no, I don't remember it at all, because there's so much in there. When I transcribed the first one, I was like, oh my gosh, I don't remember half of this.

BROUGH: I don't remember it either. I hope I don't sound insane. Like, I hope there was some reference to spirals or something?

JOHN: The concept they were talking about — I think I do remember once they talked about it more. I imagine it'll be there once I go back to the recording.

BROUGH: This Alicia or Allison or whatever — this is who I think we were calling "Penelope." I think it might be your guide. We'll have to get more information on that as time goes.

Hold on, they're giving me a couple of instructions for next time. They want you to know that there's flexibility, that you don't have to commit to this, but are you free on Tuesday?

JOHN: I have the girls, um…

[*This seems slightly odd that they are asking to meet on a specific day. Are some days better for them than others? I also think they would be aware of my weekly schedule with my kids.*]

BROUGH: Okay, no worries, let me ask them if there's another date. We may not have to do it in person either. It's nice to do it in person, but it's not overly necessary. I could call you on Tuesday if that's their preference. I could call you after the girls are in bed.

[*More conversation.*]

BROUGH: We always have synchronicity with this stuff. With Graham Hancock, instrumentation, and so on. It felt like they wanted to carry on, like there's a fluidity between conversations. Like we're doing fifty things, joking about stuff, watching people on Periscope, getting drunk, but then they go right back to where they left off before.

JOHN: And that's how it worked with Seth. He would continue exactly where he left off. It's like they're in a different time level.

[*I'm referring to Seth, an entity channelled by Jane Roberts in the 1960s and '70s. I found one of her books,* The Nature of Personal Reality, *at a garage sale in the early 2000s.*]

BROUGH: Like that idea of watching a video of a rose bloom and having the whole film and you can skip to any scene you want, any singular image on the roll of film. Where the rose is already everything, it's a seed and bloomed at the same time, in their world. They can just look at it from any angle in time. That was a very interesting concept to me. But I don't have time to ponder it, because I have to keep channelling.

JOHN: Well, that's the great thing, is that once we have it in book form, you can read it at your leisure. You'll be the first person to read it.

BROUGH: Then I'll be blown away! I'll be like, "Wow, I'm brilliant!" But it's not me at all.

JOHN: No, well, it's to do with you though. It's not entirely you, but it's you; you're part of it.

[*More conversation.*]

BROUGH: We're going to have a definition, a spiritual definition, of evolution. Which is what Darwin did in the physical form, with physical evolution. Like a spiritual Darwinism if you will.

JOHN: And yet, not Darwinism really.

BROUGH: No, because it can't be about survival of the fittest, because everything survives no matter what.

JOHN: It's not about competition, it's not about one thing winning over another thing. It's about development. Whereas Darwinian evolution says that genes change randomly and then the changes that give a survival advantage carry on to the next generation. So the changes themselves are random. Whereas what they were talking about is definitely not random.

BROUGH: No, and with this concept of a spiral, I think it starts small and keeps getting bigger and bigger and bigger. And spirit wants to extend itself, from what they told us. And to what end — to end separation, I suppose?

JOHN: Maybe no end.

BROUGH: Maybe no end, yeah. But these gaps or these schisms in the universe is what it is pulled toward, almost. That's what drives spirit to continue to evolve, that's what they said.

JOHN: To heal the separations. So you're thinking once they've done all the healing, they don't have to grow anymore, sort of thing.

BROUGH: Or, it'll never be all done, or whatever the case may be.

JOHN: Maybe that's part of growth — is constantly gathering things together.

[*Pause.*]

BROUGH: I just hear, I don't know if I could say *x*, it's like I just *heard* a smile. Like they're just, "Yeah you're getting it, keep going. Well done." Like, they believe in us, big time. You wouldn't hire a couple of clowns to fix the john, would ya?

But this woman that never came, she would have been like an older kind of psychic person, and she would have been more in control. But you know how we are, we're like two clowns bouncing off each other and the walls — *WAHHH!* And we've been like this for ten years, and apparently in half the time she would have been able to whip us in shape and get to this point.

JOHN: Yeah, she'd be like a schoolmarm. I felt sad about that because it made me think, *Well, who is she?*

BROUGH: Well, just as our personalities are a little difficult to tame, she's so stubborn, she wasn't listening to the symbols and signs to come to us. She may have seen my website; she may have had more than one opportunity and she just ignored it.

JOHN: I wonder how she was told about us.

BROUGH: Probably the same way we were — coincidences, synchronicities.

[*Pause.*]

And they're telling me that the reason the clients aren't coming forward as much right now is because this is important. They're making room.

JOHN: This is the feeling I've been getting. Sometimes they have to cut off one tap in order to get you to go to another source. Because if it keeps coming in, you know you can do it in your sleep almost.

One thing I've learned in the job world is that if you coast, things are going to change, even if you haven't consciously made them change. They're just going to change anyway. And throw you into a new challenge. And yeah, this is a challenge for you. It's something new.

BROUGH: Yeah. I don't normally channel information that isn't for a particular person. Like you said, I'm normally talking to a person about their life and they can say yes or no, and I can get immediate gratification, confirmation of my abilities, and then move on to the next point. But this is not going to do that, I'm not going to have anybody saying yes, no, maybe so.

JOHN: And it's bigger concepts that you need to interpret in your mind.

BROUGH: Well, yes — but I don't actually have to interpret anything in channelling. But *afterwards*, yeah, I do interpret. The difference is, I'm not giving a reading on a person. In a sense I'm giving a reading on the world or on life itself. You're speaking to a bigger entity.

But the teaching about evolution — this might even be one of many chapters or it might be the entire message, I don't know yet — but bringing a teaching of this kind of stuff to the world, to the spiritual community anyway, I think it's a good *reminder*.

Because I hear a lot of New Agey spiritual people being like, "We are always whole, we are always one." Which is true on a level, but to remember that there's a growth period, there's an evolutionary period, a personal evolution. You have to become a big enough person to handle the notion of being at one with everything.

JOHN: Yeah, we've always rejected simplistic, easy-to-digest, clichéd notions.

BROUGH: Not that they aren't true, it's just, tell us how!

JOHN: People have a tendency to grab on to simplifications of things, just simple little ideas. Like when people say, "It is what it is." Really. Does that help anything? Or, "Everything happens for a reason." Well, okay, yes, but even that—

BROUGH: They're saying that to avoid analyzing the situation. That's the reason they're saying that. Oh, you're right, everything does happen for a reason! You don't want to talk about this, so you're giving me a deflective statement.

JOHN: It's little mottos.

BROUGH: Isms. But a good spiritual teaching will show you the steps. Anyway, I don't want us to get carried away. I need to remain clear; I don't want to overanalyze these things. I don't want to put any of my spin on it.

JOHN: We can talk about it, though. It's important for us to grasp it.

With the Current

A new media opportunity came along for Brough. He was contacted by W5, a long-running mainstream investigative news show, described on its website as "the most-watched documentary program in Canada." They were doing an investigative piece on fraud in the psychic profession and they saw Brough as someone whose abilities were not easy to dismiss, in contrast to the psychics they were investigating.

The investigation involved an undercover reporter covertly filming readings with psychics who were suspected of using fraudulent tactics to encourage people to develop a dependency on them. For Brough's segment, they would film him doing a reading in his apartment and interview him and his client separately. They asked him to find a client that would be seen as established, successful, level-headed — not prone to superstition. Brough agreed to take part.

The client Brough chose was Dr. Christian Smith, a molecular biologist at the Hospital for Sick Children in Toronto. Brough had read him once before, two years previously. Dr. Smith was interested in psychic ability, and his mother had been a practising medium. He took an enquiring approach and hadn't fully made his mind up on the reality of afterlife, but he was open at least to the idea of telepathy.

I stayed over at Brough's the night before the filming. The crew arrived in the morning and set up lights, microphones, and cameras in the alcove where he did his readings. Dr. Smith entered, and he and Brough sat down to do a reading on camera. In the reading, Brough told Dr. Smith that he (Dr. Smith) was currently working on a book about his mother, and that he was getting this information from his mother's father, who was named George. Dr. Smith confirmed he was working on this book and that his maternal grandfather was named George. Brough told Dr. Smith that his grandfather's sister, Dotty, was with his grandfather. Dr. Smith responded with a "Whoa" and confirmed that his great-aunt was named Dorothy and went by Dotty. The members of the crew glanced at each other.

Dr. Smith told Brough off-camera that he had listened back to his audio recording of the first reading Brough had done for him before coming to the filming and that the information Brough had picked up on in this reading had not been revealed in the first reading, by Brough or by Dr. Smith. They had no contact after the first reading.

After the reading they interviewed Brough. One of the questions was "Do charlatan psychics give the good ones a bad name?" I chimed in, saying that this would be true in any field, including journalism. They told us the show would air in the coming weeks. Brough and I went for lunch at the pub and then attempted a session. Probably because of all the activity of the filming, I didn't feel the "link" there. Brough said he didn't know if it was going to work and that he didn't want me to be upset or disappointed if it didn't. The next transcript picks up our conversation at that point.

JOHN: I don't want you to ever feel there's any disappointment on my part if it doesn't work. It's not like that.

[*A few minutes go by with no words.*]

BROUGH: I just keep getting, like, they're um … just tuning me or attuning me. I don't know if it's for today; it almost feels like a developmental thing. 'Cause I'm going deeper than normal. I just went hypnagogic for a moment; I was having the beginnings of dreams. So it might be that they're putting me in that direction.

[*Taking a lot of deep rapid breaths.*]

It isn't going to happen today.

JOHN: Okay.

BROUGH: I don't think it's because they're not here or capable, I think it's because, you know, I'm tired.

JOHN: We had a lot of stuff going on today.

BROUGH: Yeah, a lot of cool stuff. So I'm distracted. But they're using the opportunity of us reaching out to sort of calibrate something, or work with me more on the connection.

JOHN: Okay. That's good.

BROUGH: They want you to prepare questions about a topic you're interested in for the next one.

JOHN: Oh! Okay.

BROUGH: It can be about something we were covering that you think is relevant, almost like a follow-up to what you've been writing out, if you think it's relevant. Like, if you have questions to re-examine about something they've talked about. For them to elaborate, for the process of writing.

JOHN: Yeah. Okay, that's good. I'll go back through what we did. I'll finish the transcript from the last one and I'll just go back through everything and come up with some things.

BROUGH: 'Cause we're gonna go back to it again — they're giving us a lecture, but they want you to — every few sessions they're going to wrap up with whatever you feel is relevant to ask. For clarity. 'Cause it'll come out better in a book. But *more so* for your understanding. Like, do you want to clarify this or that or what have you.

JOHN: Yes, okay, that's good.

BROUGH: Sorry! That must have been boring. How long was I out?

JOHN: Ten minutes, max.

BROUGH: Shit. Aw, I wanted to do it.

JOHN: I don't feel it myself. The last couple times before this, I felt that I was tuning in as well.

BROUGH: Yeah, like you have the presence.

JOHN: I can feel it. And this time I just feel we're just … we're tired, you know. That was a lot, doing the news thing. And, you know, we didn't sleep that much.

BROUGH: No. And they're sensitive to that. Like, I can feel it, but very faint. And they're doing something else with me. They were just calibrating me.

JOHN: Yes. Which is important, obviously. It's like a maintenance day.

BROUGH: Mm-hm. Tune up the ol' pickup. Pop the hood.

JOHN: Yeah. Grease the engine a bit.

BROUGH: Mr. Lube.

JOHN: I want to use your gym today.

BROUGH: I won't join you. I have too much alcohol in my system, so it's dangerous. I can't work out until I get healthy.

*　*　*

A few days later we got together for a session in the evening after I was done work. I had worked on questions the night before.

With this get-together, I found that the mind-bending information network I had found myself inside of, through vivid synchronicities over the past fifteen years, was now directly interconnected with the channelling sessions. Things would happen during my day leading up to the session that would somehow tie in with the event.

I had begun to see synchronicities as transmissions, using experiential reality itself as the medium. The transmission would consist of a sequence of points in which a theme was repeated. Each point built up to form a pattern that could be made out by the receiving person. I found that the channelling sessions would become anchor points for these transmissions, and I would experience themes leading up to the session.

That day at work I had been at a presentation in the auditorium with a giant wall-sized screen. The presenter used a "tip of the iceberg" analogy and showed a side view of an iceberg with a small tip above the waterline and a massive body underneath. I didn't mention this to Brough — there was no reason to.

On the way to the apartment, I passed a guy playing guitar and singing. As I walked by, he stopped playing because he needed to tune his guitar. I listened to how he was tuning it; instead of individual notes, he played a chord and adjusted the tuning based on how the chord was sounding. When he started singing again, I caught the word "circuit."

The concepts of "tuning" and "circuits" had been floating around regularly in the few days leading up. In our second session a couple of weeks before, I had referred to *synchronicity* as "a completion of a circuit, in which nature, our environment, is communicating information to us. And so the source is then communicating with the product."

Brough, channelling, responded with, "Yes. Again, patterns at levels much higher than you can see with your limited scope becoming revealed to you."

A week before, I had been struggling with tuning one of my guitars and I did some research on why it wouldn't tune properly. At about this same time, my daughter's band instructor asked if I could help with tuning the kids' guitars at an upcoming show. This is usually how it goes — a theme gets sprinkled into different areas of experience.

I looked around on Wikipedia: "The simplest tuner consists of an inductor and capacitor connected in parallel ... This creates a resonant circuit." Also, "a radio transmitter is an electronic circuit which transforms electric power from a battery or electrical mains into a radio frequency."

After I arrived at his place, Brough and I talked about when we should start the session. We talked about doing it right away and then going to pick up some food for dinner. But something felt off about that. I said to him, "Let's go for a walk, get food, have dinner, and try then."

I was starting to get a sense of when the particular feeling was there for our channelling to work. It was simply a feeling. We needed to hang out a bit, loosen up and connect. Essentially, we had to resonate with each other and form a circuit, or a guitar chord.

We walked over to the Sobey's market a few blocks away. Brough had a few spots in his neighbourhood radius that he frequented. Sobey's and The Granite were the two main ones. The Granite had fireplaces, pretty good food, and they brewed their own beer, which you could take home after. At both places, he knew the people who worked there. Some became clients, some became friends.

Brough seems like he can be an anti-social misanthrope, but in fact people are usually drawn to talk to him and he often gets them laughing with jokes and self-deprecation. He stays in a lot, but his job involves hours of counselling people on their most intimate matters.

At Sobey's we hunted around for what to cook for dinner. Brough usually had an idea of what he wanted to get, but this time he didn't have any ideas. I asked him what he felt inspired to get. We walked around and he started looking at soup. We discovered these packs that are basically just ingredients for a homemade soup, and you add broth and vegetables.

Back at the apartment, Brough made the soup and we watched a Chelsea Handler show on the topic of race. By then I felt the energy was there — by just going about regular activities together, we had tuned in to each other and were forming a circuit that was ready to receive transmission.

Brough lay down on the couch. Within a few minutes, he had it coming through, and we got into a wide-ranging dialogue on topics such as relationships, inner growth, and the relationship between the physical world and spirit world.

BROUGH: Yeah, I'm definitely feeling physically affected 'cause it's like I'm feeling the way you would feel if you were up till three a.m., like you're really tired, but it's not a fatigue tired, it's like a rest-your-eyes tired. And I mean, I have no reason, I slept in today, so it doesn't make sense.

I feel a very jovial, very happy energy, and it's like, "Hello! Hey, JT!"

[*His voice slows down and begins to exhibit more focused intent.*]

It's like … they're saying hello to you and they're congratulating you on making yourself available for this process. It is not just anyone who would completely put themselves aside to make time for something like this. It's amazing how much dead people have to say, and yet how few people will listen.

Of course, they need also a dedicated medium, and they always knew that they had made a good choice in selecting us to take part in this mission.

JOHN: I consider it a privilege.

[*I feel a bit awkward, not sure what to say.*]

BROUGH: They're showing me … there's three presences right now. One of which is a spirit guide. I think it's Laron, but there's three presences right now. Laron has been selected, or asked, in a sense, to join in on this and to become a potential contributor for future channellings.

They have a personal message: They want you to know that your job is more secure than you think and that, in roughly four months' time, you should be finding positive opportunities coming as a result of your current path at work.

[*This proved to be true. My contract at work was extended and I ended up being hired full time.*]

As it were, you will be sustained, you will be sustainable in the future. And they're proud of you for not worrying too much about these things, leaving things up to fate, as it were. Nonetheless, you're conscientious.

[*Brough's voice slows down further and becomes calmer, with a greater feeling of intention behind it.*]

VOICE: And we want you to know that this is the beginning of a relationship that will be facilitated between us. One that will be in long and good standing throughout decades to come. We will not leave you. We are not flippant about these sorts of things. As so many people in your world seem to casually meet and grow tired of one another. It almost seems as their tastes change, the people that they surround themselves with change as well.

We of course are very selective about our friends. But in all seriousness, we take this effort that you have put forth very seriously: We take it, as it were, to our heart.

Going back to relationship, of course; all relationship is a reflection of growth. Much like in your world, as you grow and begin to reach inner depths and understand yourselves from levels previously unthought of, you will find that through what you may call "coincidence," which is really "higher order," you begin to synchronistically encounter and connect with new people, or seemingly new people, and in another perspective you realize that they are old friends. Almost as if the deeper you encounter yourself, the more you will reflect that in the relationships around you, and the deeper your relationships will grow.

It's a common experience in your world, that children who go to school together and see each other five days out of the week remain friends for many years, but then when they grow up and leave school and assume greater responsibility in the world, they tend to not keep in touch, typically speaking. Save for a number of special cases.

Of course, this, too, is a reflection of what we are saying, that the deeper you become, the more in touch with yourselves you become;

you finally graduate from flippant relationships into deeper interconnectedness with others. After all, you can only treat others as well or as poorly as you treat yourselves. This is an unbreakable law.

This is harkening back to the conversation in weeks prior about evolution and growth. Of course, we are not speaking of your Darwinian concepts; when we address "growth," we are speaking on a metaphysical level. Inner growth, as it were. This is something that Laron has been a great teacher and advocate of for many years, through Brough, to his clients.

We wish to clarify one thing — that growth is synonymous with "change," as you would call it. Indeed, much as a seedling eventually pierces and breaks through the ground or the earth, much as a chick or a snake will pierce through the ovular egg and break into the light of the world, when you shed your physical body, indeed, it is much like a birthing process, where you have outgrown the necessity of physicality for this time. And you step into a brand-new world. One that is as yet unbeknownst to you, that you may not see with your physical senses, which does not mean it is not there, for there are many things that you cannot see, which still exist.

There are many people who have never seen a snowflake. Does that mean that snow does not exist? For the spiritual realms are real and constant, and they do interact with your world. And much like great explorers of times begone, those of you who reach up to us and request assistance and request our knowledge will find that you find us.

There are various bird species that your Darwin did not know existed until he travelled, until he made the journey. Until he took the excursion to find them and document them and study them. It is the height of closed-mindedness, the height of narrow-sightedness, for a person to claim that something does not exist without having explored it.

Indeed, we laugh in our world at those who say that we do not exist. As much as if someone were to walk up to you and call you a purple elephant, you would not take offence; it is clear that you are not a purple elephant. But you must have patience, tolerance, and forgiveness. You must become teachers and demonstrate those things to those who have difficulty accepting these types of concepts. For there is a reason they cannot accept these concepts: *fear*.

You see, for a person who has based their entire life and their entire comfort on what they can physically see, hear, taste, touch, and experience, to then tell them that it is only the beginning, that it is only the surface of the iceberg, and indeed, deep within, deep underneath the surface, there is a substantial aspect of existence, it threatens them, as there are people who equate safety with control and knowledge.

[*I get a tingly feeling as I remember the iceberg presentation at work.*]

They do not like to understand or conceive of the fact that they do not know everything. It makes them uncomfortable.

Many of your great scientists, who are currently with us in our world, postulated ideas and concepts of which there was no physical evidence in their time. Take for example, Einstein, who could conceive of black holes before telescopes could see any kind of evidence of such phenomena. All of this was found through his inner work. All of this was conceived of in his mind and later proven to be true, after his death, when your first deep-space telescopes could see the evidence of these black holes through the plumes of matter and energy that jet out into space.

You see, you are made of stars. You are interconnected with your own universe. And as you go within to understand yourself and to undo your own inner prejudice, the result will always be a clear-sightedness about the universe. Almost a clairvoyance, if you will.

Those who wish to avoid themselves and distract themselves, those who do not live an examined life, are as blind as the proverbial bat to the real goings-on around them.

Growth and change are synonymous and a constant. But you mustn't forget that you, too, can play a part in growth in that you can accelerate it or even appear to bring it to an apparent stop. Although it will never fully stop, you can substantially slow its progress by going into an unhealthy kind of denial.

There must always be balance. Whereas the momentum of life and growth and change move forward, it is always helpful if you paddle your arms and kick your legs and swim with the current — rather than those who try to turn back against the current and resist it. They find themselves paddling much harder, more vigorously, feeling frustration and hopelessness as they are inevitably carried forward, ultimately smashing into rocks and branches along the river of life.

Instead, those who do their inner homework, those who bother to reach within to understand themselves — and thus others and nature itself — find themselves like jubilant children, paddling forward along with the current, able to steer themselves more easily through the trials and tribulations of life.

These are the ones who understand the laws of nature.

Anyway, it was not my intention to ramble. You do have questions? Would you like to proceed?

[*I feel slightly nervous and unsure, realizing that I'm actually talking to a mind on the other side, and I feel a bit disorganized with my questions.*]

JOHN: Sure. Let me just get — I had some things written down, so I'll just go get them. And I didn't think that was rambling at all.

VOICE: Mm-hm.

JOHN: So, I was going through, I've been transcribing our sessions. We've had three so far. We tried a fourth but I think we just really didn't have the energy for it.

VOICE: Ah, we gave you a break. Brough did not have much sleep that night.

JOHN: No, that's right, he didn't have much sleep, and then he had to do an interview and a reading on camera.

VOICE: We were quite impressed. His psychic skills are very well honed.

JOHN: Yes. I was impressed too. I thought it was really good.

So I was going through the material so far and thinking about some of the key concepts that we've been talking about. And I would say two of the key concepts so far — the one is evolution and growth, and the other one is the concept of separation, the perception of separation, and I guess they're related ideas. And so what I did was sort of separated it into old ways of seeing things and maybe a new way of seeing things.

Whereas the old way of looking at evolution and growth would, I suppose, be the Darwinian way.

VOICE: Yes, a good old-fashioned fight. Which I might point out is in and of itself a separation idea.

JOHN: Right.

[*I pause, unsure if they want to continue speaking.*]

VOICE: Please continue.

JOHN: And advancement and growth is driven by the drive to survive and compete, according to that view, and is not guided; it's essentially a product of randomness that only appears to be non-random. And it's saying, the only guide there is unconscious physical forces, so it's sort of saying these random physical forces that exist for no particular reason that we know — and they guide this competitive evolution — and that's how we got to where we are, through this type of competition.

So, it doesn't really make a lot of scientific sense, or any kind of sense really. But it's the tale that people have come up with.

VOICE: Yes, of course, of course.

JOHN: And I guess, the new view that that could be replaced with is this idea of evolution through organic growth and development as a basic principle inherent in everything. Whereas the fully developed thing, or being, is there from the beginning and revealed through its development. And, as you said, rather than a linear slope, a line, it's more of a spiral from the centre out.

So, is this a key principle of any world, this idea of growth? You were saying it's the same on your side, and I would think it manifests itself in different ways in different levels.

VOICE: Yes. We were talking about universal concepts, which means, these truths are true everywhere on all levels. Now in your world, the reason why the idea of "competitive" has taken precedence as a theme is because, if you do believe that death is the end and that you are the epitome of existence and there is nothing more, then it would *appear* that the purpose of life is to survive. However, because you survive regardless of whether you're in a body or not, that is not the purpose of life.

Scientific theories are not always based on truth: They are highly influenced by perception. And perception in and of itself is flawed. You might take the term "perception" and put it next to the term "knowledge" and see the two as completely and entirely antithetical to one another. For perception is based on limited perspective. Perception is akin to trying to observe a masterpiece work of art through the small hole of a straw whereas knowledge is where you have taken off the straw and gazed at the entire picture.

However, in linear three-dimensional and four-dimensional time, you are indeed seeing this universe through the tiny lens of your physicality. But you, as a soul, are much, much larger than the body. Though indeed growth and evolution are, in some regards, predestined paradoxes, predesigned by the mind at a higher level that you are not conscious of.

You would be surprised how everything that appears to go on in your life and in your world had been set into motion from the very moment of the big bang. The first spark of the universe itself. And indeed our world serves as a skeletal framework or a coat hanger, a blueprint as it were, that every force in your universe, every planet, every body, every rock, every grain of dust, every molecule is guided and led by the subtler dimensions of the spirit worlds.

The main message, of course, behind this is that you are not lost, you are not alone. This is why people who refuse to look within, people who live a life of distraction, with materialism, objectification, and selfishness — not in the sense of looking within but in the sense of only preserving their own interests — find themselves quite disconnected and quite out of touch, as it were, with reality.

But again, we encourage understanding and forgiveness and compassion, for those people are frightened. They're frightened of who they really are and what they really are. To be big, to be bigger than a body, to be eternal is, after all, a *great deal* of responsibility.

Suddenly, once you grasp the concept of eternal life, you realize you have to live with yourself forever. Many, many souls, who are in a soul sleep as it were, who are living unconscious lives, are terrified of having to face the idea of existing forever. Because they are then accountable for everything they say and think and do. And this is a burden that they feel they cannot bear.

Many people would prefer to believe that everything is meaningless, and they are free to do and say whatever it is that they want. And on the other side of the same coin, there are many people who do believe in a spiritual existence but who have given themselves a personal mission in your world, to carry out the wishes of a wrathful, vengeful deity. Which, by the way — the very notion of being an angry god — is laughable to us.

Take for example your movies on Earth. If you have watched a movie ten times plus and you know exactly how it begins and exactly how it ends, you do not have emotional reactions to it. Those of us who are very advanced in spirit already know the patterns and the way the story plays out in this world. It is not a shocker to us, as it were, or a surprise.

Rather we attempt to intercede and to break bonds of suffering and pain, to lighten the load of your life, to show you gently and with wisdom, potentials of a better way. In other words, to assist in this spiral growth of yours, to take you deeper within yourselves, to get deeper and closer to the core of your being so that you might be able to connect with each other and others. This includes animals and all the way down to insects. To make of yourselves guardians of life, protectorates of the sanctity of life, great teachers of peace and harmony.

But again, this is why we must commend you for your journey and your willingness to explore. For you take this for granted about yourselves. Most people in your world prefer to live in a numb malaise, to never break free of their shell, to never look up and take a peek at the real world around them.

Many people, their lives become about clothing, the shoes that they wear, the distractions that they cause. This concept of "vacations" in your world is quite funny to us. Where so many people are already out to lunch all the time. But you literally fly across the planet to stay in resorts that resemble your actual homes, watch television, sit by in-ground pools that you have in your own backyards. Whereas few people actually travel and immerse themselves in other cultures. The very notion of such is seen as unsafe, frightening; indeed, this points back to the fact that most people in your world have separated themselves *from* themselves. And thus find it impossible — in other words, they segregate themselves from the rest instead of seeking to find commonality in the human experience and the beauty and difference.

You call this lapping in luxury, and we see it as a very narrow vision, a very closed mind. Meanwhile, fewer and fewer of those beautiful cultures are able to exist. Indeed, nature is being bulldozed and replaced with desolation.

This is quite a state the world's in, but don't worry. Humanity does not have the power to destroy it. Nature always finds a way. And there are many, many, many souls coming into your world who are going to be a part of a spiritual relief act. Engineers, technologists, even politicians: The future generations will consist of many activists and free thinkers that will be dealing with the restoration of balance in nature.

The next three hundred years of humanity will focus greatly on the healing of the planet. There is much hope and many good days ahead.

Would you like to speak?

JOHN: Well, that's very good to hear.

Now the second concept, maybe it's sort of an offshoot of the first one, but there is the perception of separation that you commented on that exists in people, and if that's the old way of viewing things, that could be replaced by the concepts of "diversification" and "variety" and "creativity," whereas things grow and change into new forms. Rather than seeing that as things separating, it's more about growth into new forms that all remain interconnected. Is that a truer way of seeing what we perceive as separation?

VOICE: You are, as Brough would say, bang on. We stated earlier in another conversation that the word "matter" might as well be replaced with the word "mirror," which you appreciated. Indeed, as things evolve, as things grow, as things develop — to see yourself in those things, is true wisdom.

But the true separation is within yourself. Those who do not live an examined life will find it quite easy to point out differences, whereas those who learn to seek within, to examine themselves, as it were, are able to clearly see the interconnectedness of this world. It requires no special meditation, no special course. Just a healthy reminder that you are interconnected with the universe; and therefore, you must spend some time throughout your day thinking about how and why it is that you behave and think and say and do the things that you do.

Indeed, everything begins with thought. Thought translates to words, which translate to deeds. Pay attention to your deeds, your words, and your thoughts. And ask yourself where they truly came from. And you will start to notice that some of the things that you think and say and do were things that you had been taught, or *mis*taught by poor teachers. Whereas other things that you think and say and do had been taught to you from kind and good and wise teachers. And it will become apparent to you that the things taught by the wise and kind and good teachers always consistently led to positive outcomes in your life.

And indeed, it is the wisdom you wish to choose. Before you can do that, you have to identify the false teachings you have been given and you have to take action to undo them. The action that you would take, simply put, is to start by being vigilant of your thoughts. Identify the negative thought patterns that lead to negative experience in your life. And in the moment where you catch yourself having that negative thought, stop and breathe and make a new decision based on health and healing and interconnectedness and compassion. Both for yourself first and then for others.

And you will find, slowly, the false teachings you have been given will become undone, much like pulling the thread of a knitted sweater. And as you begin to undo negative thought patterns, your entire life will begin to change. At the risk of oversimplifying things, this is the basis of many helpful, therapeutic techniques and teachings in your world.

And as we said, our resident expert, Laron, is quite a psychological expert. It may interest you to know, John, that she just winked at you.

JOHN: I was just picturing the photograph of her, in my mind.

VOICE: Hm. She wants to say to you, JT, that you are a very good friend to Brough. And that you are an excellent father. She is impressed by the benevolence of your parenting techniques.

JOHN: Thank you.

VOICE: It is not easy having rambunctious children. The tendency is always to blame parenting, but genetics has a huge role. Your live-and-let-live philosophy of acceptance, an unconditional form of acceptance, is quite advanced.

Finding balance between creating boundaries — healthy ones — and accepting, is a very delicate process and a complex one. And you do it with very specific deliberation. You put much thought into this. And it's not something you discuss verbally with people. But we can see this in your actions and in your thoughts. And we are very proud of you.

For on your deathbed, your children will hang off of you like puppies. It will be a testament to how loved you are and how good a job you have done. Never forget that.

Laron has leaned in and given you a kiss. Apparently, you are a ladies' man both in your world and the next.

[*This gives me a laugh.*]

JOHN: I'm blushing. Thank you for those comments; it's very moving.

VOICE: Laron is very attentive, she pays attention. Those who have been selected to be life guides are experts in the humanities. You know, Laron was a victim of the Holocaust.

She doesn't speak much about this. However, having been so affected in her last physical incarnation, she has devoted her existence to assistance and guidance of those on Earth. Oftentimes those who have been afflicted by such violence, and the idea of separation in your world, could not be any better demonstrated than the idea that one group of people is superior on some level to another group. For whatever reason.

The souls who agreed to carry out those experiences are often great teachers of the humanities, teachers of life. And in many ways, her purpose is fulfilled through the mediumship of Brough. To heal as many broken hearts as possible and assist people gently in making more well-informed decisions. To affect the direction of their lives and the decisions they make, day in and day out.

What we aim to do here is educate. For it has often been said in your world that knowledge is power. And the end of terrorism and the end of subjugation and the end of suffering is always going to come from education. And education is another symbol of self-actualization; to go within and to reveal deep inner truths about self allows you to clear away the fog of amnesia so that you may peer out toward the stars and understand the universe itself, with clarity and wisdom.

You can only accomplish this once you've gone within. There is no other way. This is an important message right now in Earth history because, now more than ever, the technologies being developed, the so-called modern conveniences of your lives, serve as excellent distractions.

We're not against technology, we are against the misuse of technology. Technology is very helpful and useful; indeed, you are using it to record our very conversation. Remember there are many other uses for computers. We find this to be an apt use.

As they say, it is not about the sophistication of your weapons, it is about the warrior who wields them. Any use of technology to facilitate deeper connection with self — and thus promote an interconnectedness with others, a fellowship as it were — is a high, high use.

Whereas most people today use these technologies to distract themselves from exactly those things, those goals which matter. And others use technology to further a dastardly cause, to organize great, ruthless campaigns to further separate and subjugate from others and toward others.

For everything, there is a correct use and an incorrect use. And we postulate, we pose, that those who go within first will look inside themselves and examine the root of their behaviours and their thoughts, their deeds, and words. Those individuals will become clearer channels to use the tools at their disposal correctly and facilitate freedom and growth and happiness and peace. How few and how far in between.

You have more questions for us? The link is going to be closing soon.

JOHN: What just popped into my head when you were talking about the use of technology was, I've seen recently a lot is being achieved in changing the treatment of animals that are farmed for food, through campaigns on the internet mostly, I think, petitions and social media being used to pressure companies. And to me this seems like a very important step for our civilization, to make that change and acknowledge animals as having rights and not just being there for production of food. So I just wanted to bring up that topic as being a very positive step that I see happening.

VOICE: Yes indeed, there was a time, for many, many, many generations, where the people of Earth lived in harmony with animals, and although they did use animals for food and they did use animals for clothing and they used animals for farming, there was a respect of those animals. Many of them were allowed to carry out happy lives.

This mass farming, this mass production of animals, and this cultural and societal view that they are not sentient beings couldn't be further from the truth. Greed, selfishness, desire for material gain, and the distraction from being connected to nature has led humanity down a stray path where it has begun to abuse its animals. And indeed it is an epidemic.

Every single day, in our world, people who are dying from self-imposed poor health arrive in our side of life. And there's unspoken shame that's carried with these individuals, much like the shame of people who commit suicide.

We had hoped you would notice that your decisions in the dinner that you created tonight were influenced by us. Every time Brough was trying to think of what to make, he could not think of anything other than soup. And we guided your eyes to notice that packet on the shelf. And how fitting a question you would ask, as we had guided you to make healthier and vegetarian-based decisions.

Humanity has the technology to thrive and survive in a healthy way without consuming animal flesh in the form that you do. And it is not far off before you can molecularly create a meat-like product without even having to put a life form through birth and death and subjugation in between.

Just as you currently have the ability to give up fossil fuel. But only when enough people are doing their inner homework and connecting with self will they be able to see themselves in nature and the benefit of taking care of the whole system. And as a result of that movement, which will occur eventually, each individual will no longer consume unhealthy food, creating themselves to be disfigured, with dis-proportionate amounts of fat, and wreaking havoc on their internal systems until they essentially send themselves over to our side. This unintentional suicide. Which is a reflection of a disconnect with self.

When you look into the eyes of a cow or a pig, you will find that you can see yourself in those eyes, you can see a soul in those eyes, you can see feeling in those eyes. There are many in your world that already experience this, but there are many more who genuinely believe that there is no intelligence, no soul, no sentience, no emotion, no feeling with these creatures. We pose that those individuals are often the ones who do abuse others. And to cover up their own guilt, they have to tell themselves that those things that they abuse have no feeling. It makes them feel better, you see.

There are many problems in your world that have gotten out of hand, and nobody, no individual, wants to take responsibility. Those who work in slaughterhouses, those who work in waste plants, those who work at the forefront of devastation are merely doing their jobs. And those who are in control never visit the farms, never visit the dumps, never visit the rainforests. They sit in cushy offices. They see themselves as simple financiers. It's a convenient system that everyone remains disconnected, that everyone remains unresponsible. And this convenient denial allows for the system to continue.

But whenever and wherever there is a soul that is aware, that steps in to speak out and to draw attention to the very thing that every individual participating in the system does not want to look at, those souls come under ridicule. Because if someone has spent their entire life trying to avoid looking at something they feel is wrong deep inside, that they feel guilty for, the moment that someone, an activist, comes along and shines a light on that ugly little truth that you haven't been looking at, your natural ego response will be to attack them, to break the light that is exposing the inconvenient truth.

But the more activists there are, the more teachers that exist, the more people willing to stand up and shine a light on the inconvenient truths, those that have been able to get away with self-denial for so long will no longer be able, will find themselves having a tireless sleep at night. And one by one, slowly change begins to happen, and reconnection begins to form.

In the future, these practices of mass farming and devastation of land will be looked at much like how you look at your own Holocaust, that Laron had been a victim of. It will be the holocaust of the world. And the future generations in the next thousand years won't judge. They'll simply see a society of people in pain. People who did not know any better, like children, who eventually grew up. Which brings us back to the original concept of growth, of course.

We will be bidding you good night soon, but we wish for you to congratulate yourselves, give yourselves pats on the back. For as you have grown and developed and you have maintained a close bond of friendship and sibling-like brotherly love, you have also bonded with us. And through those bonds and through your growth, this relationship is possible. And you will be teachers and ambassadors of spirit and of love — to pave the way and to help people who are seeking a better existence to find their way and to find their calling. For this we thank you and we will be with you.

Take care.

JOHN: Thank you.

BROUGH: [*Sighs, still lying on the couch.*] Ah, I started to get a headache. I was getting a piercing in my temple, which is different. I never get headaches, ever. I'm not a headache person.

JOHN: That was incredibly strong and powerful — like, clear.

BROUGH: I felt heavy eyelids, like, it felt really nice when I closed my eyes. And that man, 'cause it's a man — Laron is, like, right there, and I can feel her — but the man that was speaking was like a figurehead, probably one of the main … not your spirit guide, he's like a guy, who is like an advanced being of some kind.

JOHN: So there was a male, a man speaking?

BROUGH: That was the one speaking, the man.

JOHN: And is that different from previous times?

BROUGH: No, it was always him.

JOHN: Oh.

[*This surprises me, as I didn't realize he was perceiving a gender attached to the speaker.*]

BROUGH: But he's an advanced being, and he is, in his sense, a channeller too — because he's speaking about a bigger deity, like, he's channelling love. The way that I channelled love. And then Laron and your guide with the "A" name, she's there, but then there was another person, there was three of them.

JOHN: Principal communicators, they were saying.

BROUGH: Yeah, principal communicators. It's like a big seance. It's like all of us are teaming up so that we can all channel love, a bigger concept.

What did you think? I don't remember everything, 'cause I don't think, eh, I just *blublublub,* like if I'm in a reading.

JOHN: It's amazing watching and listening to you.

BROUGH: Is it redundant crap?

JOHN: No ... no.

BROUGH: Okay. That's all I'm worried about. If it's grammatically crappy, throw it away. I'm not gonna believe it if they don't know how to speak.

JOHN: No, no, no. I mean, there's the odd little—

BROUGH: I think that's the glitch in channelling.

JOHN: I don't think that matters at all. I mean, it's 99 percent perfect in that way.

BROUGH: Well, that's high praise 'cause it's gotta come through me to some degree, so it won't be perfect.

JOHN: No, I only notice the odd little thing, and to me that's extremely trivial because it's very clear that there's something very coherent coming through.

BROUGH: One thing I noticed was that it was very consistent with bringing it back to growth and evolution. And I couldn't believe the tangents and the sophisticated details that it was going through, that could almost make you think that it was changing the subject, but it always came back to growth. To the point where I was even thinking, "Oh God, where are we going with this? This can't be them, this can't be real, now I'm just blah blah blah." But then it always came back.

JOHN: So, you're kind of observing it while you're doing it.

BROUGH: Yeah. But I don't even hear the thought first. It just comes out of my mouth.

JOHN: Yeah, it's absolutely incredible how that's happening. I mean, it's just so strong. And it just started right away, as soon as we sat down.

It's just amazing — it just goes like a train. And I was just so happy to just listen. There's just no doubt in my mind. I almost never have any thoughts of, "Hey what is this? Is this just Brough?" It just comes on like a locomotive, and it's coherent, you're not pausing to think of what to say. It's like a book is just coming out.

BROUGH: Yeah. Like they pre-plan what they wanna say. And I'm telling you, whatever I do when I'm doing a reading on a client, I don't know what I'm going to say to them, I just go. I don't even have to think.

JOHN: So, the thoughts aren't there and then you're translating them. It's just there.

BROUGH: Right out. I'm almost surprised to hear what's coming out. I'm listening with you.

JOHN: And the things you're saying to me about parenting and everything, these specific things about the girls.

BROUGH: You and I have never talked about that. We've been friends how long, but you've never talked about your parenting with me. It's something that Laron made me feel you are extremely private about, and I want to say there's a sanctity, you're very protective. Those aren't the right words — but it's a sacred thing for you. You're not a religious person or an overly spiritual person — you *are* spiritual, but — that is sacred and untouchable for you. And Laron, I think with the collaboration of your spirit guide, wanted to validate some inner feeling or philosophy of yours. Was it true, though? Did it make sense?

JOHN: Yeah, yeah. But again, it's not something I would really consciously plan out, but yeah, that's how I do things. I try to find that balance between—

BROUGH: Benevolence and boundaries.

JOHN: Yeah — letting them just develop their own natural way of being.

BROUGH: And doing what you can to not intercede or interfere with that. Or influence it one way or another. To let a rose become a rose.

Are you seeing it all tying into other stuff, from previous sessions?

JOHN: So, this one did tie into previous sessions. This one was a little — is "angry" the word? It was giving Earth people a piece of their mind.

BROUGH: Yeah, I know what you're saying — the word is … assertive.

JOHN: Or indignant.

BROUGH: We're not pussyfooting around here. Let's get down to brass tacks. Confronting — confrontational but not in a conflict way. In a "let's look at this" way. Like they said, shining light on the inconvenient truths.

JOHN: Right. And that surprised me 'cause the previous sessions weren't to that degree like that.

BROUGH: I think they wanted to establish where it was coming from first. That's why the previous sessions were like, this is love and this is what the fundamental spiritual problem is — disconnection. And what growth is really a symbol of. Growth is not so much becoming something else; growth is becoming what you always were. It's like a remembrance. And then this — "now let's get down to Earth" stuff. Let's talk about the nitty gritty now.

[*More conversation.*]

BROUGH: I just heard, just now, it's like, "Hold on to your horses, kids. We're just getting started." It's gonna go into politics, it's gonna go into the way in which people operate in the world and how that's a direct reflection of the way we operate within ourselves. To simplify it, the message is gonna be, *If every individual person learned to do their own inner work, the whole world would change overnight.*

There's no way around that; that has to happen.

The Highest Form of Light

Our next session was ten days later on a Sunday morning. As usual I stayed over on the couch the night before. Brough had a reading scheduled so we only had a window of about an hour. We planned to try again after the reading but didn't get to it. In this session, our entity went deeper into aspects of the relationship between self and others, including some delving into my and Brough's personal lives, and some counsel on the dynamics of our partnership. Finally, out of the blue, we were mysteriously guided to … a YouTube video.

We assumed our usual positions and Brough had contact within a few minutes.

BROUGH: Ah, there they are. Got the loving presence encroaching.

They've just shown me a clairvoyant image of a triangle with each point with a circle on it, and the triangle's sort of rotating counter-clockwise. I can't tell if that is an attempt to get me to focus on something — and now it's turned into a star. I'm actually seeing the image on my closed eyelids, it's not in my forehead as usual. It's an actual projection, like a screen, like my eyelids are a screen.

Hm, they've just informed me that they're going to be putting healing energy into me. And instructing me to relax. There's that voice again.

VOICE: We are here, we are with you. Good morning.

JOHN: Good morning.

VOICE: We understand that you did not have much time to prepare as detailed a list as you usually would. But we believe you have three concepts that you have contemplated. How would you like to proceed? Would you like to ask questions or would you like us to communicate to you free will?

JOHN: Um, I think I'd be happy for you to start off, and then if you'd like we can get into some of my questions?

VOICE: Of course.

Of course, you know that we follow you and your progress, spiritually, on the Earth plane. And your personal lives are very much known to us. What you call "privacy" does not exist in our world. As such we would like to discuss the concept of "relationships" today; both relationship with self and, by extension, with others.

We of course relate to you, as guides — as "soul worker" could replace the term "social worker" in your world. We care deeply for your progress and for your well-being. Our modus operandi being that growth continues even on our side.

Through the service that we provide you, we ourselves learn valuable lessons that aid us in our exploration of reality. Deeper, more fundamental levels of existence become apparent to us through the work that we give, the service we do — which we will get into, the dynamics of how such things work, at a later date.

It is not necessary in relationships for both parties to be equally aware. There are many in your world who believe that in order to have a successful relationship, both individuals must share interests and commonalities, thought systems, political views, goals, aspirations, in common. Of course, this is not so.

Anyone who has been in love romantically and is with a life partner can attest to the fact that they are not merely with that person for their interests; there is a deeper connection, an ineffable connection, one where you feel akin and at one with the person. An inexplicable familiarity and a deep yearning.

[*Authors' note: Instead of "ineffable" in the preceding paragraph, the word "ephemeral" was originally used. Since the definition of "ephemeral" is "lasting a very short time" it clearly didn't fit with what was being said. When I raised this during book production, Brough went back in his memory to when he delivered the passage and said that word originally intended was "ineffable," which means "too great or extreme to be expressed or described in words." Whether the error in word choice in a case like this is attributable to the Voice or to Brough himself, would be worth a future discussion.*]

Spiritual guides find you in much the same way. For whatever reason, when someone has chosen to be a guide, to follow the workings of those on Earth, it is very much like falling in love.

Find a child — often between the ages of newborn baby, sometimes even as early as still in the mother's womb, to the age of three — and you will watch them grow, guide them, comfort them. Indeed, many spirit guides even appear to children, take the form also of a small child, where they are able to form a companionship, a bond of trust.

Oftentimes as the physical brain continues to grow and develop, the child's psychic abilities are often deactivated. Early-born children have a different chemistry in their brain, which allows the frontal lobes into the visual cortex to go quiet, almost as if the child were meditating. And these things can happen when the child daydreams or plays with their toys in their room. And it is this quieting of the frontal lobes that allows us to project telepathically.

Other children, such as this medium, Brough, grow past their youth and are still able to quiet their mind, in a very natural but genetically induced way. And this is what you will call a "psychic." For Brough is fond of an analogy we once gave to him through thought transference, that indeed the stars are always shining, but when the distracting light from the sun is in the sky, you cannot see them.

But surely as the day is to end, when the sun sets and its light no longer fills the sky, one by one, gradually and quite beautifully, each star twinkles into existence, as if it were born anew. Indeed, when you practise meditation and learn to quiet your frontal lobes, one by one, we will become apparent to you, and our world and dimension will slowly twinkle into your point of view.

But we are like the stars, we are always shining, regardless of whether you can see us or not. Many, many people have seen spirit in their youth and have forgotten or repressed such memories after being told that that was imagination. Rest assured, it was not. We are with you.

And as we grow and learn on our side — through your experiences and through helping you — you, too, are able to live a more productive existence, protected from potential disaster through your intuitive senses. For many people have had the experience of driving too fast and suddenly getting the sense of impending doom and slowing down only to find out that a police officer was just around the next corner.

[*I find this example kind of funny because the impending doom is getting a speeding ticket, not being in a car accident.*]

How often do these experiences go unnoticed and forgotten? Where these are the exact experiences of spirit intervention, working to keep you safe and steadfast on your mission.

Spiritual guides are not relatives. They are not blood relatives; they are not people that you have been acquainted with on the Earth plane. They are people who have, as I said, followed you from your early childhood years, and through some inexplicable attraction — connection — chose to aid and assist you on your journey.

Not all those on our side choose to be spiritual guides; let me be clear about this. It is a task that some are guided to do. There are no governments, no social organizations that dictate purpose to us. For without physical dependencies, we have no need for governing agency.

Each soul is free to determine their own function and purpose in the greater scheme, which is a luxury that you do not have, for very important reasons pertaining to the need for social structure and support in a physical universe.

Although we do not agree with the way everything is run in your world, for the most part we understand the needs of the physical. And guides work tirelessly, quite literally, to help inspire change when and where change is needed for the greater whole. After all, the spirit in which agencies and structure in your world are built directly stems from the need for physical survival and protection from the elements. How few people in power remember that truth.

In much the same way, we connect to you, even from another dimensional plane. When you find yourself drawn to and connecting to a new friend, a possible lover or a child or an animal for that matter, do not write this off as wishful thinking or codependency. Although those things are truths in your world, the type of connection I speak of is *soul* connection.

It can be said that although human beings rely on a physical aspect for love to exist, that love also has a spiritual component. Indeed, primarily a spiritual component. Two souls who connect always connect first on our level and then find each other yet again in the physical.

It has been said before that everything you see in the natural universe is a symbol of a higher reality. Think for a moment about your star soul, the sun, and its relationship with its system of planets, which orbit it. It could even be said that the friends you meet in this life, and lovers that you make, are a part of a soul system.

Of course, some planets orbiting farther from the central star, which is you, whilst other planets orbit much closer, all equally important and serving a function. Where if people were to think of relationships in this manner, not only would they be closer to the truth but they would certainly be able to appreciate each other more.

Since your recent space probe was able to send images of the planet Pluto back to you, in a very comedic way we have noticed a growing number of Pluto supporters and Pluto sympathizers, a great number of people feeling quite badly that Pluto is not listed as a planet.

Is this projected sympathy not applicable to our relationship lives? How many of us have been guilty of thinking of only a certain group of people, a certain type of person, as worthy of our attention and our time and our energy. Whilst other more peripheral individuals remain unworthy of that same affection and regard.

You see, for us the epitome of a healthy mind is consistency. An enlightened person is one who treats strangers with as much regard and respect and sympathy as they would a best friend or a soul mate. For as you think of Pluto, think of those acquaintances and passers-by who do not have a chance to see you very often, perhaps only once in a lifetime, and hold them and cherish them with more respect.

The benefits to your psychological and emotional health will be great. As you begin to treat everyone equally, you are sending a message to your unconscious mind that you are equally deserving of the same respect and love and regard. For you see, what you believe about others is ultimately what you believe about yourself. This is a truth that cannot be escaped.

Of course, what we are suggesting is not that you should love and be kind to someone who is harming you or who is a danger to themselves and others. What we are suggesting is purely a different point of view; to think about others in a kind manner, but then to act accordingly.

It is not our desire for you to go behaving strangely in your world. Our words should not be taken as some literal symbol that you should go and hug a stranger. That would frighten people, and that hug would be false. We are merely suggesting that you pay attention to how you think and regard others mentally.

Where if you were to meet one of the advanced beings on our side, you would notice that their gaze, the way that they look at you, is full of love. A loving gaze from across a room can have a greater impact on a person than a physical touch.

A mind that is healthy and whole and consistent and regards everyone with equality is an irresistible and magnetic feature. For every other mind that is broken and split will be inexplicably attracted to a whole mind, a healed mind. Almost without realizing why. As a moth is to the moon.

Please feel free to pose your questions; we'll do our best. The channel is a little weak today.

JOHN: Thank you; that was very strong material, though. I did feel things were a little bit weak, maybe for both Brough and I this morning, but still some really amazing material came through anyway.

VOICE: A chef is only as good as his ingredients.

JOHN: That's good! [*Laughing.*]

VOICE: We are catching up with Brough's humour, you see.

JOHN: A very apt joke for Brough.

The relationship idea and everything you're talking about is pretty relevant to the things I had written.

VOICE: Yes, we are glad you noticed that.

JOHN: Which in turn, the fact that that was relevant, also plays into what I wanted to talk about, just that everything seems to be connected, that we're doing. I mean you probably know that I have notebooks of ideas that I've written down over the last seven or eight years, and a lot of this lines up with the thinking I was doing, and I imagine that a lot of the thinking I was doing was inspired in turn by you.

VOICE: Correct.

JOHN: At some point I want to go back through all the things I had written down and bring some of those things forward. A lot of the ideas were inspired by the synchronicities I was having, which led to me meeting Brough. And I've noticed while we've been doing these sessions, I'm having synchronicities with the sessions, and I feel there's some intention coming from your side in making those synchronicities happen.

VOICE: All true.

JOHN: As an example, the iceberg analogy in the last session — I pointed this out to Brough and sent him the picture — you know I had been in a meeting at work, there was a presentation, and one of the slides in the presentation was an image of an iceberg, and I stared at that for quite a while. And then that same night came over here and you used the "surface of the iceberg" analogy.

Also the Holocaust, talking about the Holocaust in the last session as well — and I don't know if I've expressed it to Brough this way before, but the mass farming and so on, I've often compared that to a holocaust. And, you made that—

VOICE: Of course, this ties into what we were just speaking about. You are an example of a very advanced mind, for you can see the equality and the deserving of love and respect, even for animals.

[*This throws me off, being told I have a very advanced mind. I pause for a moment.*]

JOHN: Thank you. And then it just amazed me because I was typing that session up, and it ended with the part in which you explained how, in the future, this period would be seen as a holocaust of the world. And then I went to work the next morning, and a co-worker was saying her friend was a producer on a documentary on the Holocaust that was just nominated for an Oscar.

[*The documentary is* Claude Lanzmann: Spectres of the Shoah, *and is about the making of* Shoah, *which itself was a twelve-hour Holocaust documentary.*]

So I'm seeing all of these interconnections, these things happening, that adds a whole other dimension to the work we're doing. I'm not sure how to describe it, but it shows the whole thing as kind of a larger structure that we've formed, I think, with Brough and I, between our minds, and your minds on your side. It seems we've formed kind of a super-structure.

VOICE: A latticework, as it were.

JOHN: Yes. And so, I guess that was what I wanted to bring up and get your thoughts on.

VOICE: Absolutely. There will be those who read this book and believe that everyone can channel. Indeed, everyone is channelling, in a sense, their own mind. As you are not inherently a physical being.

The physical aspect of life is merely an extension of a representation of the desire to explore all levels of reality. Not everyone is capable of channelling in the form that we are doing with this work.

There are many people who believe that they are channelling, and we stand by and we attempt for a time to feed useful information to them. But the filters that they have — their belief systems, things they have read in books and forgotten — seem to funnel through them. And they end up being a closed circuit, producing very little relevant information.

As you know, Brough is an accomplished medium in your world. Many thousands know of him and have come to him over the years. And it is his work as a medium that has allowed him to be an appropriate channel for higher information.

He is not speaking with ego when he has criticized channellers. Often pointing out that well-known channellers in the past, whose names we will not mention, had never done readings and never developed as a psychic before yet were somehow responsible for channelling advanced information. We do not dispute that they were gifted channellers and that that information was pretty good.

[*When saying "pretty good," the tone is more one of being impressed than of sounding dismissive.*]

But ultimately an accomplished medium is the most well suited for revealing information from our side to yours. You know of the medium David Thompson, who has developed as a physical medium, which is another form of channelling. Most people reading this book won't understand what physical mediumship is.

So for the purpose of explanation, I will briefly explain that it is when a medium is able to go into a full trance, and the spirit guides extract ectoplasm from the medium's bloodstream, bringing the plasm out through an orifice, say an ear or an eye socket or a nostril, often the mouth, and then spirit constructs a voice box that they can speak through, and voices then appear out of thin air in the room. This does happen, as fantastical as it may sound, and it does take years and years of development to accomplish.

David Thompson is capable of the exact kind of channelling that you and Brough are doing right now. His spirit guide, William, has often spoken directly through him, using his own body. Indeed, that is the first form of trance that David had undergone before becoming a physical medium.

Each group of souls, each circle, both on our side and on your side, has its own set of principles and its own mission. Where we felt it would be more important to assist you in your collaboration was to construct and create a book that will come in handy and be useful, not only for yourselves but for anyone who would care to read and become seekers on the path of enlightenment.

As we have said before, we hold both you and Brough in high regard. We are often laughing with you when you cannot even hear us.

JOHN: That's nice to hear.

[*I often wonder if they enjoy our humour. I think they may be pausing, waiting for me to say more here. But I am very engrossed and not ready to say much.*]

VOICE: Getting back to some of the perceptions people will have about this work. We would like to take this opportunity to remind them that you and Brough have been developing for twelve years plus now. We did not, as you might say, pick you out of a cereal box. Brough is an accomplished medium, and you are an accomplished technician. This was no accident.

Stand by.

[*Pause.*]

And so, we wish to convey, in this chapter, the purpose of relationship. You had mentioned a structure, or latticework, which is a very technical description for our relationship and an apt one, I might add.

We were talking about how it is important to endeavour to regard even strangers on the street with as much respect and kindness as you would your soul mate. For this is a key to finally learning to love yourself.

It is often said in your world that you must love yourself before you can allow others to love you — this is true. But the problem with such an analogy, or a saying, is that they never tell you how. I am about to do so.

Your subconscious mind is an endless recordkeeper, a perfect stenographer, masterfully memorizing every thought, every deed, every nuance, every word you hear, everything you see, keeping it buried as the iceberg remains under the surface of the water. And within that scope of all those thoughts and all those images forms a core belief about who and what you are.

Only when you reach to your higher mind, or spiritual mind — which you are also unconscious of most of the time — using your *carnal* mind, the one that you see and think with from day to day, can you begin to funnel down, from the higher realms, spiritual truth into your subconscious. Imagine for a moment a break in the clouds and a beam of sunlight shining through. When spiritual truth enters your mind, this is what happens on the subconscious level.

Using your day-to-day carnal mind — the one you are seeing through right now, reading these words — learn to look at others with love, compassion, understanding, sympathy, respect. And that crack into your subconscious void will fill with light. And the truth of your own worthiness, of your own value, will shine through deep within your soul.

And for the first time ever, what you have always wanted, often not even knowing it, will become yours. You will feel worthy. After all, someone who goes around loving everyone all day can't be half bad, can they.

This is the secret to mastering self-love. You cannot love yourself until you have given equal love to all. So, on this day, make a pact, an agreement with yourself. That you will endeavour to think differently from now on.

You will not excuse bad behaviours, you will not allow abuse, and you will be guided to intercede when you see an injustice in the world, but all the while thinking to yourself, "That person must be in pain to be doing such a horrific thing. I wish for them that they could experience love and rise above their surreptitious acts."

For it is possible to disagree and still respect a person. Something that is far too seldom experienced in your world, we feel. Perhaps you shall correct us if we are wrong. We dare you to.

Please continue with your questions. The time runs short.

[*I am surprised by their saying, "We dare you to." I'm not sure if they are referring to any of my personal situations or behaviours.*]

JOHN: Sure. Well, yeah, I mean, I have difficulty with a person in my life that I love very much, but then I feel she engages in destructive behaviour towards me and herself. And I'm always torn about how to support her but without taking abuse from her, and we have this cycle we go through where I try to help, but then I'm pushed away again.

VOICE: Yes. Of course, we are aware of this situation in your life, and we support you endlessly, you know that.

Those who consistently do not know how to love others, in essence do not love themselves. Those who do not love themselves will, in turn, project their inner hatred out onto others, eventually. In short, she is not ready for the kind of connection that you are ready for. There have been many songs written of this, many tales told, many poems in your world. It is called unrequited love.

Eventually, hopefully, with some careful guidance, she will wake up, and her behaviours will heal and change — no one is beyond grace. What you must learn from this lesson is the concept of "boundaries." Healthy boundaries. And it is a great opportunity to examine yourself and ask yourself why it is that you feel personally responsible to save another, who is fully capable of saving themselves.

For your well-being, we hope eventually you'll decide to put some distance, temporarily, between you and the other. And that when they speak to you, from an objective point of view, because of the distance you have put, you will be more free to tell them exactly what you think.

The closer you become connected to a person, it seems the less they take you seriously because they know your flaws. And it is an unfortunate truth that people discredit each other out of insecurity. Which is why the dynamics we are describing and the thought system we are prescribing to you is a cure for that insecurity and inequity within yourselves.

Earlier we had said that successful relationships do not require that both people are on the same page. Indeed, it is true; it only takes one master to heal a couple. Tell her that you love her. Tell her that her patterns are self-destructive. And tell her in a number of months you'll have an excellent book to recommend her.

But there is no need for you to personally take on mental or emotional or spiritual abuse. For although you are indestructible, the only reason you do take responsibility is because on some level, you do not feel worthy of being treated well or properly.

Brough's spirit guide, Laron, has taken a special interest in you and your well-being and has some interesting psychological information for you for a later time. Perhaps you'll consult Brough about this.

JOHN: I definitely will. Thank you, and you helped confirm some of the things I was already thinking.

VOICE: You're welcome.

JOHN: I liked what you were saying about Pluto, and I noticed that in the images of Pluto, it had a heart shape on it. And I, of course, always see these things as synchronistic, and this isolated forlorn planet, cast out of our solar system, our hierarchy of planets, and then when we find it a couple years later, it has a symbol of love on it.

VOICE: Yes, how many of you have Plutos in your soul systems. Peripheral connections that you do not call, that you do not reach out to, that you do not respect. That you keep at a distance. This type of human behaviour stems ultimately from a sense of materialism. One could even categorize this as acute materialism.

In other words, those who go through life like opportunists, only looking for what serves their immediate needs and not thinking of a higher picture, look at friends and acquaintances and people based on neediness.

It could also be said they are using others to construct a temple of bodies to worship them. The Plutos always being the people who are of least value to you. Ironically, it is often the people who would be of most spiritual value who are lumped into this category.

We have spoken briefly of your relationship life. We are going to speak of Brough's for a moment. It is very difficult in your world, although, in this part of the world — Canada, North America — acceptance toward homosexuals is much more common than it used to be. It is still very difficult for homosexual people.

And as a result of living lives of adversity and difficulty, many young homosexual people carry shame in their subconscious mind. Which leads them to be very self-defensive, ultimately materialistic.

They regard looks far too much. One would say they regard looks over health. Appearance over quality. Many of them objectify each other, using each other for mere stimulation — sexual or even less healthy forms of stimulation, such as drugs, alcohol. Poisons.

All the while overlooking the value of deep connection. This is why Brough does not have many gay friends. For he has played a Pluto in the lives of many. His spiritual teachings do not appeal to people who are not ready for them.

We remind Brough that it has often been said in Christian communities that a preacher's own parish never accepts him. He must go to another city. That is why the demographic reading this book are not going to be largely homosexual males. Although Brough may very well possess fundamental cures for his entire culture, it is sad to see that none will listen.

[*A note from Brough: This passage is speaking in generalities, but I believe there is some truth there. I have long pondered why it seems so many of my gay and lesbian peers experience more anxiety and higher rates of substance use, and many have shorter-lived relationships. The Voice's explanation of being caught in a survival mode, leading to long-term anxiety disorders, makes a lot of sense to me.*

Of course, the statement about demographics of the book does not mean that gay people aren't supposed to be reading this book. We intend to revisit this topic in a future book in greater depth, and I have been assured psychically that we will have further insights and answers for marginalized people specifically.]

Do you have a question to finish up our session?

JOHN: I don't think I have a question particularly ... I think what I want to start doing is taking more time to digest the material that's come through, and as you probably know, I just got a printer, and I want to print everything out so Brough and I can really sit down with it and read it. And then I can spend a little more time coming up with things from my end to really get the most out of what we're doing.

VOICE: Yes, we see your dedication to the project. It is nothing but inspiring.

We wish to bring up a subject, and you must understand: Thought form is not the same thing as direct telepathy. The words you use in your mind are not always things we can hear and sense but forms of thought we can see and experience quite physically.

You and Brough love each other like brothers but often disagree with and judge each other. This is not conducive to our project.

We are going to task you with some homework, to be more openly communicative with one another. It will feel raw, vulnerable, and frightening at first. But it will lead to a very deep bond and a mutual respect that will assist in the contact field. By no means are we asking for you to be perfect. And we are not asking for you to feel bullied or pushed by one another. We're merely asking for clear communication.

[*"Contact field" is a term used by instrumental transcommunication groups. It refers to the ability to establish communication with the other side. In our case it refers to mental mediumship rather than technological mediumship. With ITC, it is thought that the strength of a group's contact field is determined by the degree of harmony and cohesiveness among the members of the group.*]

We indeed were the ones who told Brough that it would be useful to collect and put pictures into this book. We are aware that you are resistant to this idea. But the reason behind our inspiration is because the information is already very fantastical for the average reader, which is who we intend to reach.

We realize, because you are the ones living this information, it is natural and reasonable for you, makes sense to you. But for the average layman, who we intend to reach, seeing photographs of your misadventures together will solidify the idea in their minds that you are real people and that this information is coming from a genuine collaboration. It was not thought up or contrived.

We realize mere photographs are not to be considered evidence. But it does personalize the material, you understand. When Brough seems forceful, it is often not his fault; we must take the blame. With an idea that has been plunked into his head, so to speak, like an excited puppy, he will take the bone and run with it.

Indeed, he could do a better job of being clear that it is spiritual information he is presenting. But of course, his fear with that approach will be that those around him, whom he respects and loves, will then accuse him of using his psychic ability as an excuse to get his way. You see, Brough is very sensitive.

But we wish for you to use photography in this book. Both of you are artists, in your own regards, and it will be appropriate for you to stylize your pages and invite the reader to be a part of your relationship.

Again, we are merely guides. You do not have to listen to us. If for some reason you feel that our suggestions have no merit, well, we will defer to your choices. But of course, it seems hardly intuitive, as your intention for writing this manuscript is to convey ideas from spirit. Why would you then curtail our ideas?

Unlike Brough, we have no qualms with being pushy. For we have a perspective that you lack. You must think of us like your elders. When your mother told you to eat broccoli, and you resisted, it is much the same situation with us. We are often telling you to do good things for yourselves, and you are often resisting. And it is only the fact that we love you that we are inspired to tell you these things and make these suggestions.

[This is very surprising to me and I find it discouraging. I am planning to use photographs in the book, and I emailed Brough about it. I told him that we could use my printer to prototype books and include pictures.

This raises the question with me of how they interpret our thought forms. I did have dismissive thoughts about one photograph Brough wanted to include, in which I thought I looked vacant. I didn't express these thoughts at the time, as we were emailing and I was at work.

Are they picking up on this one negative thought and applying it to the whole topic of photographs? It seems like a misunderstanding. I feel a bit scolded.

Still, the point about Brough and I communicating more honestly is a crucial one, and I will remember it.]

Of course, we understand that there is so little expression of genuine love in your world, that it is hard for you to trust love. Indeed, most of you believe that love is a subjective thing. It is not. Love is a vibrational frequency. It is the top of the spectrum, the highest form of light.

And as human beings, all creatures have the ability to tap into that spectrum. There is a famous video on the internet that neither of you have seen. You will have to look it up.

A father is filming a windowsill ledge and explaining to his son about the harsh realities of physical life, as a bumblebee is caught in a spider's web. Suddenly the most unexpected thing occurs. Another bumblebee swoops in and rescues his friend, snatching him from the spider's grasp.

This incredibly, immeasurably rare event was specifically guided by the higher vibrational frequency of love. The odds required for the fellow bee, flying through the air, to be in the right place at the right time, to notice its friend, and to be guided to swoop down and break him free is a task that only the frequencies of love could accomplish through such a small creature.

As human beings are now equipped with more cameras, meaningful and beautiful acts of love like this can be seen all throughout the animal kingdom. They were always happening; there are simply more cameras now to capture it.

You are not alone. Until next time.

JOHN: Thank you.

BROUGH: Have you seen this video? I haven't.

JOHN: No, I haven't heard of it.

BROUGH: I want to find out if it's real. They should have given us a YouTube link.

JOHN: Yeah. I mean, that would be a pretty amazing video. We'll have to find it.

BROUGH: How would we even look it up?

JOHN: Oh, you just put in the right search terms, I guess. Shouldn't be too hard to find it if it's out there. Just a bit of searching should find it.

[*Some discussion about the session.*]

BROUGH: Is it true, did you have some doubts about pictures?

JOHN: Actually, I was going to bring that up because I don't at all. But maybe, when we were emailing this week, there was a picture you wanted to use, and I didn't think it was very relevant. The specific picture that you wanted to put in, I think.

BROUGH: Oh, they caught a form of your thought. Like they said, they can't read the thought, but they can see the form.

JOHN: Yeah, I was resistant about that one picture. So, they caught that thought form, I guess.

[*I find this quite fascinating, that they aren't necessarily omniscient and that there is still some interpretation involved on their part. I raise this with them later on.*]

A lot of the things they're saying, it helps me trust my intuitions because it lines up exactly with things I've been thinking. About women, about you, and everything. Like how they're saying you'll suddenly get really excited about an idea, and I might be like, whoa where's this coming from? And you don't want to say that it's something that you've psychically received. And I totally get that — that made so much sense, about how you don't want to bandy that about, as the idea having more authority.

BROUGH: It's also a tall order to expect friends to go with my psychic stuff. With clients, everything I say is inspired to *them* because the boundaries are there. They're my client; I'm only sitting with them to service them psychically.

Friends don't have that boundary.

JOHN: It was interesting because they were getting more personal with us.

BROUGH: I have a feeling they're going to get more personal as time goes on.

I remember them talking about David Thompson. And I was cheering inside when they were saying not anyone can fucking do this. Saying Brough has been a practising medium for seventeen years. That stands for something. They gave us credit — they're saying, "We didn't just pick you out of a cereal box."

JOHN: Well, it's funny because they referred to you being a great medium and me being a great technician, which I might want to talk to them more about in the future. What is a technician? Do I fix things?

* * *

Later that day I found the video on YouTube by searching "bee spider rescue." It's titled "Bumblebee in spider's web rescued by other bumblebee." Posted in 2015, on a YouTube account called FunTV, the video is narrated by a man with a British accent and captures an incredible encounter between two bumblebees and a spider. The image track shows a bee caught in a spiderweb, being filmed from inside a window. The narrator explains that he started recording the bee's struggle on his phone as a "sort of brutal life lesson" for his son. While he was filming, a second bumblebee crashed into the web and rescued the first one by stinging the spider. Slowed down, you can see the attack, including what looks like a stinger extending into the spider and retracting. As the narrator explains,

> Bumblebees don't die when they sting, by the way, that's honeybees.
>
> So did the first bee somehow communicate its distress to the second? Or could it be just chance? It's pretty rare to see two bumblebees together. Bee experts, please tell us. I caught the two bees afterwards and released them out the window. But I couldn't find that spider anywhere.

The existence of this video, which neither of us had heard of, and the fact that it was almost exactly as described, with the father filming it to show his son a life lesson, freaked us out.

Contacting Your Guide

We had our next session about a week later. In the morning on the day of our session, Brough had an out-of-body experience involving his mother. These experiences were not uncommon for him. They usually happened early in the morning when he was lying in bed. He would feel vibrations and then float up and out of his body and fly out the window. He said, "it's like the landscape outside transforms and I'm in the spirit world."

In this case, it started with him feeling three pokes on his rear, which felt physically real. This reminded me of our early session where I was awoken by three audible claps. Brough floated up and out the window, where he found his mother in a Victorian mansion. He recently described this experience in conversation with me:

> I was there in her mansion and then she said, "Go find your room." Laron was there too, and she showed me where my room was. Mom was in the main area, sitting at some kind of screen. Not a computer as we'd understand it. On the couch in my room was a small deformed kitten, face hadn't formed fully, didn't have eyes. Then my mother's voice said, "You have to heal it." So I held the cat and poured all my love into it. And it started to look like my old cat, Oreo, who was living with Darby, my sister.

Then I look up and there's five men about my age and they look like the Beatles. Suits, nice clothes on, '60s-era bowl cuts. Very attractive. But they were family. Never met them, but they were family. And they said, "We're going to show you around." So we flew off and we entered this beautiful ballroom in another place, not this house. There were thousands of people, thousands of tables. Space was weird there. It would have had to be miles in space. Fit more than should fit into that building.

The boys took me over to one of the tables. Everyone was dressed in Victorian clothing. I experienced total exhilaration, excitement. I wanted to tell them what Earth had been doing in the last century. I was telling them how we went to the moon and all about the space station, the internet, cellphones. They were just laughing and smiling, just regaled. I realized as I was talking, the things I was talking about were appearing in a three-dimensional hologram in the middle of the table. It was like the table was able to read my thoughts and project them in a visual form. Then if I were to stare into the image, I would enter into the vision and be inside it. If I reoriented myself into the room, I'd be back there again.

I came back to the room and one of the boys said to me that we were in the Hall of Communication. The tables are where spirits learn to communicate with spirits on Earth. And given I am a medium, they thought it would be interesting for me to learn about this.

They took me back and I spent some time with my mom. I went back to my bedroom and the boys had to go. They all gave me a hug individually. I found myself crying because I was moved. I felt they were my brothers and I would miss them. Then Laron smiled at me and I was back in my body.

I woke up and I had tears. For five days I missed those boys, I was grieving. I was told that some of them are great-grandparents, generations of men from before me. Everybody really looks twenty over there.

After waking, Laron expanded on it. The tables are a form of technology. They use "Borynthian" waves. I received this term. This ties into the structure of the universe, part of the dark matter spectrum. They are highly reactive to thought forms. Sound waves need air. Borynthian waves would be like air, the medium, for thought. Fundamental in the structure of the universe.

Sometimes when spirit people communicate with us, they are at a table like that and they are able to be with us in some form. You can be in places through this substance somehow. Sometimes spirits are right there in the room with you, sometimes projecting from this Hall of Communication. It's like bilocation, two places at once, like a copy of the person.

Darby called up and said, a week prior, she had to put Oreo to sleep and never told me. She thought it would be too painful because I couldn't be up there. It can be argued that these things are dreams, but things like having Oreo appear without my knowing he was put down indicates it's real.

After that experience, Brough said he had been "feeling the presence" all day. I came over after work and we went for a walk, then had dinner. As we started getting ready to channel, we were getting zany. Brough received a message saying that it was best if we were jovial before the session because it created the right energy for channelling to come through. Fortunately, that was a pretty normal state for us to be in together.

This session would be epic in length and scope. We have divided it into two chapters. The first includes a step-by-step exercise for the reader, which appears as it was delivered to us in the session. This is followed by dialogue in which I am given my "professional designation" in the psychic field. We also discuss the mechanics of channelling and receive clues about the limitless possibilities open to those who take the inner road.

BROUGH: A little poke in the rump. A little "one, two, three, you're out" … out of the body, that is. Kicked my keester out of my body, she did.

Was your guide an "A" name, that we were talking about? Not Alicia, but … you can call her Alice if you want. What was the name that they said?

JOHN: You said Alice, but you weren't sure — just that it started with A-L.

BROUGH: Alessia. Alessia.

JOHN: Okay. I heard that name today though. Did you say that name earlier?

BROUGH: No.

JOHN: That's strange.

[*I think I might have heard the name at work. It's a strong déjà vu feeling.*]

BROUGH: Yeah. You would remember having the "A" symbol, a lot of the A's for you. Not to take any profundity from it, but it may have been an indication of your spirit guide as you became interested in contact.

[*Brough is referring to the dream mentioned in the first chapter, where I saw a capital A in the sky and subsequently had synchronicities relating to that.*]

JOHN: [*Gasps.*] Oh — and there was a woman in the dream, the "A" dream I had, standing next to me. She said, "Not long now."

BROUGH: Of course, that was referring to what we're doing now. And where this will lead.

[*Brough very suddenly starts to speak as* them.]

VOICE: Hello, John.

JOHN: Hello.

VOICE: As you know, it is a pleasure for us to speak with you.

As we had warned Brough, we're going to focus on some practical techniques tonight that we feel you would find very useful in the coming weeks.

By implementing the techniques that we're going to give you, we believe that not only will you be able to strengthen the connection with us but as well strengthen your own spiritual muscles. Or as we might call them, the psycho-spiritual muscle.

For just as you commit to a regimen of exercise for the physical body, to be in shape and fine working order, it is indeed necessary to commit to a regimen of psycho-spiritual practice in order for you to forge a connection with our realm and with your inner self.

The word "spirituality" could be replaced, or rather used synonymously, with the concept of your inner journey, the road within. Many people confuse spirituality with doctrine and other concepts, such as rules, and other disciplines, such as religion. But for the purpose of clarity, we wish to redefine the concept of spirituality as being "the road one takes within oneself." Nothing more and nothing less.

The prevalent theme that we've brought up in these talks is that what you notice in the world around you and what you appreciate in the world around you is directly governed by how much inner homework you do. The more self-aware you become and the more healing work you do within yourself, the healthier your relationship with the exterior world will become. This is a universal law that cannot be broken. Although many try.

Those who neglect a deeper meaning, or an examined life, find that the universe begins to close doors one at a time in their path until they are left with nothing but to face themselves. This is very typical and sometimes can take a lifetime, if not several, to happen to a person.

The more advanced that you are, it seems you cannot get away with anything. The moment you start to ignore, your doors will immediately shut on you. For those of you who feel that you cannot ever get away with anything, and luck seems to turn on you in a fraction of an instant, rejoice, for the fact is that you are too good to be bad. You are too aware to forget. You do not have the luxury of ignorance.

Your thoughts, it has been said before, have a relationship with the universe around you. Change your thinking, and your life will change. In order to strengthen this effect, meditation is absolutely essential.

[*One of Brough's cats jumps up onto his chest as he lies on the couch.*]

Ah. It has been a long time since I have felt an animal sitting on me. Marvellous.

Brough, he loves these little animals.

Meditation is a very important tool. As we alluded to earlier when we quoted something that we have had Brough say before, during his readings to clients: Just as surely as the sun goes down each day, one by one the stars begin to twinkle into view. That the stars indeed were always there, but the sun needed to get out of the way for you to see them.

When you take the time each day to go within, close your eyes, rest your body, and tune out, as it were, the world around you, surely as each star twinkles into view, subtler spiritual dimensions will begin to become apparent to you. Now this has a two-fold effect. On one hand, you will become more familiar and able to recognize the spiritual subtle dimensions, the astral plane, when it does appear in your life, even with distraction, for you become more sensitive to it.

And on another hand, you will begin to flex your psycho-spiritual faculties. They, like your muscles in your body, will begin to strengthen and grow and be able to function at a more consistent and deeper level.

[*The Voice at this point goes on to dictate the exercise that follows.*]

Exercise

We wish to give you a simple meditation technique. One that does not take much effort, and that you can practise enough to become good at doing almost anywhere in your life. Whether you have a comfortable chair to sit in or whether you prefer to do this in the morning or in the evening or in the afternoon in a bed, you want to position your body where you can completely relax every muscle group, including your neck, without the fear of your head falling forward.

Begin by resting your body and starting from the very bottoms of your feet, mentally working your way up through your ankles and your legs, your calves, your knees, your thighs, your buttocks, all the way up, relaxing each muscle group as you go; up through your pelvic area, your stomach, your lower back, your ribs, your chest, your shoulders. All the way down the tops of your arms to your lower arms and hands, releasing tension as you go, being cognizant of the fact that you must let go.

Try to keep a rhythmic breath during this proceeding. Up through your neck, paying close attention to the tightness of your jaw, around your nose, the back of your head, around your eyes, paying especially close attention to your forehead, up to the crown of your head. Relaxing every single muscle group and breathing rhythmically and deeply as you go.

At this point you will have noticed that your body begins to become itchy and fidgety. Please know that that is okay. Try to resist the temptation to itch. Try to resist the temptation to scratch. This is simply your brain becoming bored and looking to distract you, as your brain is used to a certain level of exterior stimuli. This is a good sign. If your brain is becoming bored, it means you truly are letting go of physical distraction.

The next step is a visualization technique. We want you to visualize the room that you're in filling with a white light. For some, it is helpful to imagine a waterfall or a liquid or even a gaseous state, similar to the mist that falls out of your freezer door when you open it on a hot summer's day, billowing down from the ceiling in the form of white light.

And allow that light, as you breathe, to pass through the layers of skin of your body, deep into your tissue, into your muscles, all the way through your veins, your cartilage, your bones, slowly moving down through your entire body. Until you are filled with a beautiful white light of positivity.

At this point, you will be sufficiently relaxed, and you will have practised using your visualization techniques. If you so desire, you can ask mentally for your spirit guide to impress upon you some feature or detail about themselves: their name, their gender, their appearance. Whatever you wish, ask mentally.

It can sometimes be helpful if you ask verbally before you practise this technique. Clear your mind and allow whatever comes to you. Perhaps it's a form, a shape, a letter, a whole name, a face, a smile; don't judge it, whatever it is, allow it to come. The more you practise this, the more clarity you will have in contacting your spirit guide.

As time goes on, with further practice, you can ask more complicated questions through direct thought transference. This basic meditation will serve as the template for more advanced techniques to come, including exacting instructions on how to willfully project outside your body.

Be aware that the effects that we talk of (i.e., contacting guides, projection out of the body, enhanced psychic skill) happen through a process of development. All that's required is a small willingness on your part to commit. A little each day will eventually add up.

[*After this exercise is delivered, we continue with our session.*]

VOICE: Replace the word "prototype" with "template," please.

JOHN: Um, what's that referring to? The prototype of the book?

VOICE: The sentence where we refer to this meditation specifically serving as a prototype. We meant to say serving as a template. A template for future meditations that will lead to projection outside the body.

[*I made this change later, in the transcription.*]

We believe that these techniques will greatly assist those who've been diagnosed with terminal illness. To induce out-of-body experience is of great aid to people who are facing and fearing the inevitable transition into spirit. Indeed, what comfort it could bring to have an experience similar to Brough's this morning and to reunite with your loved ones even before physical death.

We have a feeling Brough is resisting the temptation to make a joke. He feels that we are attempting to put him out of business. *Ha ha ha.*

JOHN: That's right, he'll have to learn how to work at McDonald's or something.

[*My joke is ignored.*]

VOICE: After all, perhaps he can become one of those channellers who takes his act on the road.

What wonderful concepts you have, what worldly concepts you have. You always think in the macroscopic, don't you, John.

Do you wish to start by asking questions, or lead the dialogue this evening?

JOHN: Um, sure, yeah. I had extensive notes that I left at home, but on the subway I was able to recreate them, I think, most of them.

For every session there's a million things I could go into, when I read back what was written, what was said, so I have to pick and choose of course.

VOICE: Yes, we understand that your idea is to formalize or form a first chapter using the information that is at hand. This is a very good idea; in fact, it's an excellent idea.

We wish to give you some of the techniques to begin your path into spiritual development. We believe that the meditation serves as an interesting and a good exercise to put at the end of the first chapter. Indeed, it is our intention that each chapter include at least one, if not two, unique exercises that people can practically put into use in their life.

[*The division of chapters did not always end up following where the Voice suggested they would, as we chose to go with one chapter per session in most cases.*]

JOHN: I think it's good. I could use it as a way of tuning in, I suppose?

VOICE: Yes indeed; the first step is tuning in. But when you realize your potential as a transmitter, not just a receiver, that is when they say the fun begins. And we will be getting to that eventually.

JOHN: And I was reading in my notes here earlier, I had written something about everything being a transmitter and a receiver, just on the way up here. And I had a dream once — I was being operated on and a transmitter and a receiver both were placed in my chest. Like a speaker and a microphone. Are you aware of this dream?

VOICE: Personally, I am not. But I have a sense that this dream served as your subconscious speaking to you about its foreknowledge of your work in the psychic realm. Was this dream not within five years?

JOHN: Well, it was probably a year or two after I met Brough.

VOICE: So, it would have been closer to 2005.

JOHN: Yeah, I had a series of dreams during that time that were very powerful. Definitely I would say foreshadowing what we're doing.

VOICE: Excellent. In a previous session we referred to you as a technician. Of course, any name or title you are given in this field of work falls under the umbrella of "psychical." You are a psychic technician. What a perfect and apt dream for a psychic technician.

JOHN: *Ha ha* — yeah that's right. Yeah, I was thinking of that term "technician"; at first, I thought, I'm not just a technical person, but then I thought of the different levels to it, the different meanings.

VOICE: In much the same way you can think of Brough as a healer, or an emotional surgeon. But we say these things under the umbrella of psychical. So, a psychic healer. Just as you are a psychic technician.

JOHN: As opposed to a physical doctor of some kind.

VOICE: Correct.

JOHN: Yeah, I like it, I like that. Psychic technician, that's pretty cool, *ha ha*!

VOICE: Mm-hm. Just as there are psychic teachers, just as there are psychic gardeners, psychic crime solvers. There are many different paths for psychical beings to take in this world.

We wish to reveal to you, we do not think we are spoiling any surprises by telling you, that you and Brough are meant to be teachers as well. You are very personable and good with crowds and people individually. And so, your work and your purpose to be fulfilled will definitely have a teaching component to it. And that is a discussion for another time; after all we do not wish to get ahead of ourselves.

JOHN: Yeah, I guess we'll have lots of time to cover these things. Brough was ill last time, as you know.

VOICE: Yes. He was not completely ill at the time, but we felt it best he conserved his energy.

JOHN: Right. So, he needed to conserve his energy to work at the illness. So, it requires energy from him to do this.

VOICE: Not quite. We funnel energy through him. However, in order to do that, we must slow down certain processes and certain parts of his brain and physiognomy. And for us to do so involves linking into his central and sympathetic nervous systems.

When the body is undergoing an infection and its automated systems are already sending out white blood cells and anti-viruses, for us to meddle with the body would cause further confusion and chaos and could have an unintended synergistic effect.

For example, we would not want Brough's white blood cells to begin attacking his frontal lobes and cause him to have seizures, so we must be careful and very delicate with our mediums.

[Merriam-Webster *defines "physiognomy" as "the art of discovering temperament and character from outward appearance." So I believe they intended to use "physiology."*]

JOHN: So, the changes that would be caused by going into the different state could be seen as some kind of foreign invader or something?

VOICE: Moreover, the effects that we can have on tissue could cause the body to mistake that tissue for having an invader and begin to inadvertently attack the tissue.

JOHN: So, when he's ill, basically, the best thing is for him just to rest and get better.

VOICE: Ah, is that not best advice for all who are ill?

JOHN: [*Laughs.*] Yes. Well, should he even do readings when he's feeling sick?

VOICE: Ideally not. Try telling him that.

JOHN: I will. And he feels good, not having been drinking for a few days.

VOICE: Yes, as we're very proud of.

JOHN: And do you notice that difference, for what we're doing now?

VOICE: The connection is very smooth.

JOHN: I noticed you came through immediately. Usually there's a buildup and he describes what's happening, but it was almost instantaneous this time.

VOICE: Yes. When you use a microphone too close to an amplifier and you receive feedback — it is a very similar effect with our thoughts, that when our mediums are not at peak health or when they are not attuned properly, our thoughts will bounce back to us in a screeching manner, very similar to the feedback you have with audio equipment on Earth.

So, when there's alcohol involved or any kind of substances, we do have a certain amount of mental feedback that occurs. Which can be a useful tool for us to understand what is coming through and what's not coming through — the words and nuances that reverberate back to us are things that we realize that Brough is incapable of hearing at that time. But we find another angle to say the same thing differently.

But on an evening like this, when the energy is pure and there is a body in good health, there is very little feedback.

[*This very physical description of thoughts coming back to them like feedback strikes me as incredibly interesting. While they do not live in the "physical" world as we know it, descriptions like this show that they still have some kind of external factors that they work within. It's often not until later, when I am transcribing, that I fully grasp what is being said.*]

JOHN: Do factors outside of Brough, things like weather patterns, anything like that, have an effect?

VOICE: It depends on the level from which you are channelling. From the lower astral realms and even some of the realms that human beings and their pets inhabit for several hundred years, known as the Summerland, there can be some difficulty channelling through certain mediums during heavy electrical storms due to both ionic as well as electric interference of another kind.

But for the most part, when channelling from the level from which you are tuning into now, we can come through rain or shine. Provided there is a sufficient medium present.

JOHN: Yeah, that was my feeling. It seems more dependent on Brough, and I suppose on me to some degree as well.

VOICE: Yes, of course. As we've said before, this is not something of a hobby that you boys have recently decided to pick up out of the blue. It is purposeful, to state this again in this book, that both you and Brough have been developing for over a decade. That this did not come about overnight. Because believe it or not, there will be many supporters of this work who will themselves believe that they can simply strike up a chat with us at will.

We look forward to seeing how you and Brough diplomatically handle those in the future who approach you and claim to have a message for you from us. We will stand by idly grinning as you politely listen and apply some of the spiritual techniques we have yet to teach you, to these individuals.

Always remember, it is not important to get others to agree with you, or whether or not you agree with others. The most important thing, indeed the most spiritually healthy and productive thing, is to endeavour to leave each individual feeling happier when they walk away from you than before they came. To live by that simple principle, in whatever form you can attain it, is an ideal that will catapult you light-years ahead in your spiritual development.

We want to again remind you that when we say "spiritual development," we are directly implying that your ability to perceive the universe accurately is at stake. *Spiritual awareness is synonymous with sanity.*

JOHN: Okay. Well, this plays right into what I was going to talk about. In the last session, you made some points about communication between me and Brough, and we definitely heard that. Certainly, Brough and I have had disagreements many times over the years, and we always come back together. We've had some volatile periods, and then more recently we've noticed how it's become more stable, over the last year or so.

And so, you were telling us we need to be open with each other; if there's an issue, we need to bring it out into the open and develop more honesty with each other. Which makes good sense. With anyone, of course, but especially in our situation, I guess.

VOICE: We wish to add to that. You can clarify the term "honesty" as being emotional transparency. In other words, to speak what is truly in your mind and heart without fear of judgement from your brother.

The biggest mistake we observe both you and Brough making is that you argue with each other in your heads, assuming you know what the other will say before you even bring it up to the other.

This is often the side effect of two who have a very strong psychic bond. For indeed, many of the things that we hear you saying to the other in your head are exactly what the other would say. You literally carry out arguments mentally, oftentimes without realizing that you're doing it at approximately the same time during the day. It could even become a game for you two, to point out things that you had been thinking about the other and catalogue your time.

By using emotional transparency and trust that the other one has your best interests at heart, which is something we recently reminded Brough when he was concerned overly with the use of the audio of these texts, you will realize that it will calm you down and you will be able to open up to one another about your thoughts.

We did, of course, remind Brough that John is not out to kill him. Which is a laughable notion of course, but it did calm Brough down.

JOHN: Okay. That's good. My view on that was that he was obviously having an issue with the idea. I wasn't quite sure why, but to me it wasn't that important, because if one of us doesn't want to go ahead with something, then we just don't go ahead with it. And if that person comes around, then we can go ahead with it.

VOICE: Hm, yes. If there is some idea that you have that would be truly detrimental to the project, rest assured you will hear from us. So far your ideas have been good and congruent with the intentions behind the work. We are quite pleased with you.

JOHN: Okay. I felt a little bit misunderstood in my view last time when you were saying that I had resistance to putting photographs in. You were saying that you had picked up a thought form from me on that.

This is a good opportunity to understand how you pick up on our thoughts. Because from my point of view I had always felt that I was in favour of using photographs for the same reasons that you said — that it gives people a view into us as people and into our lives, and they see us as real people.

And so Brough suggested that what had happened was he had emailed me about a particular photo, and that particular photo I don't think is a very good photo of me. So I might have had a negative reaction to the idea of using that particular photo. So, I was wondering if you could give some insight on that. Was it that I reacted to that photo, and that's what produced that impression?

VOICE: That is exactly true. Because we remind you Brough had only specified one photo, although he implied the use of others, but that was the one photo he had specified. We sensed resistance around that; we did not see the detail of your thinking.

You see we are incapable of reading your mind word for word, but we can sense thought forms. The difference is to look at a beautiful house but not know exactly what's going on inside it.

You can tell of course a few things from the silhouettes in the window; perhaps a family is just sitting to have dinner on a quiet evening. But for the most part, you cannot see every goings-on inside the mind of another. Although there are beings who can — that is a subject for another talk.

JOHN: That's absolutely fascinating. Because from our side, I might assume that, oh, you know, you would know exactly what I'm thinking at all times, kind of thing. But it's interesting to see that you have a particular way of picking up on the thoughts on our side, and that it won't necessarily give you all the details, but you'll get impressions.

VOICE: There are great teachers to whom there is no one and no thought beyond their immediate awareness. These are the teachers who have rejoined with the creative force. I myself am not going to pretend to be something that I am not.

I am an advanced being, but I am not yet an ascended teacher. In a sense, you could think of me as an older brother. I have had more experiences and gone further down the garden path than you. I can show you the way; I can give you hints and tips and survival techniques that I have learned so far. But only an ascended teacher can take you the whole way.

When you eventually get to my level, and you eventually will, there are even higher teachers. In a sense it is a bit of a game of cosmic leapfrog, in keeping with the childlike analogies.

As you begin to develop spiritually, you will find that your mind has many great powers: telepathy, psychokinesis, advanced and ultra-healing capabilities, the ability to perceive time itself —past, present, and future — and the ability to affect reality on many levels. All will become apparent to you, as well as more possible.

You can think of it a little bit like a lucid dream. When you realize in that moment that you are dreaming, you can suddenly fly or see someone that you haven't seen in years or go somewhere that you've never been, and start to control your dream. The more awake your mind becomes, the more developed you become, you will have more psychic effect in this universe.

For we stress the concept we first came through with, which is that there is no separation between you and the things that you can see and perceive. Indeed, there is only oneness.

The more you grow to accept that, the more your mind heals at levels that are beyond your conscious awareness, and you will regain access to power. But before that can happen, it is fundamental and important that you learn spiritual concepts and spiritual law. As it is possible that even the most well-intended person can abuse power.

And so, there is a steady growth that occurs. So that you, as it were, do not bite off more than you can chew. You do not feed steak to babies; you give them pablum. And as you make yourselves ready, and as you grow spiritually, you will be given more abilities and access to more powers.

But you will also find life throws more complex challenges your way. Because there is a relationship with the mind that says you will only be given what you can handle.

Your famous Mother Teresa used to have a saying — that God only gives you what you can handle. She would then look up at the ceiling and say, "I just wish he wouldn't trust me so much." You will find this to become a truism in time.

We will have to have a break in this channelling but we will commence after the break. Do you have one more question before the break?

JOHN: Oh, if we need to break that's fine. I have lots of questions but...

VOICE: Good. Keep them concealed.

[*Brough comes out of his channelling state.*]

BROUGH: Keep them concealed; don't let me see. They're letting me break 'cause I have to pee.

Blinded by the Light

We continued with the second half of our session after a few minutes. It was a wild ride. The Voice spoke of the purpose we all have in this world before drawing me into totally unexpected shared hysteria. But it wasn't over yet, because we would then go deep into a mystery from my childhood.

VOICE: We of course appreciate your questions, John. Would you like to continue?

JOHN: Oh sure, um—

VOICE: We understand that your subjects and your questions are topical to the things that we have already mentioned, which we feel will allow you to wrap up many concepts for your first chapter. This is a very good idea on your part.

JOHN: Yeah, I do feel sometimes certain things need a follow-up, before we move on, I guess.

VOICE: By all means: *Follow. Up.*

[*At the time I don't understand why "follow up" is being emphasized so deliberately, and I feel like they might be teasing me for using a business-like term. I get a bit nervous. Later on, I realize they were probably making a play on words, referring to following guidance from "up there."]*

JOHN: At the start of the last session, Brough had a mental image of a triangle. Then we were talking about relationships and so on. It was a triangle with a circle on each corner, and it was rotating slowly, and then it developed into a star. Later, we talked about the latticework, and this seemed to me like an image of the latticework — the psychic latticework forming, formed, between us as a group.

VOICE: Yes, that is a very good — and technical — description for the clairvoyant image that we facilitated. Of course, you remember at that time, Brough was having a mild anxiety attack, and we were using clairvoyant imagery to pacify him and help him focus.

Having said that, your interpretation of the shapes we chose is very, very good. After all, the shapes we chose are tied into our psyche as well. We chose a certain symmetrical shape where all sides are equal; for with circles and triangles there are no asymmetrical bits. And it was our intention that this symmetry was to focus Brough's mind so that he would further calm down, and his heart rate would slow.

However, that does not take away from any of your interpretation. Because we feel your interpretation is absolutely correct. There is indeed a psychic latticework between our souls. Would you like to expand on that idea?

JOHN: I guess I do have this feeling of a network that links together all of our thoughts and shows up in the basic synchronicities that happen, that link up with the work that we're doing, which I've said before, so…

VOICE: A good way to think of it is that advanced souls, some of whom reside in the physical world — and of course there are those over on our side who are advanced — have the power to link and cause an interconnectedness among a small group of souls. A network, as you call it.

This of course is yet another one of those abilities that become unlocked for everyone as they advance. It is another symbol of interconnectedness, as we have alluded to, that spirit's sole function is to affirm oneness and connection. That separation is merely an illusion in the presence of spirit, as shadow is to light.

[*Brough coughs a few times while talking.*]

JOHN: Do you need water?

VOICE: No.

So, as I was saying, the more advanced souls, without consciously realizing it, tend to serve as hubs, or central...

[*Here Brough tries to find the exact word intended, before going back into channelling.*]

BROUGH: I don't have the word for it ... I'm trying to listen to the word; hold on. It's like a post, they're showing me a big post. Transmitter? No. No, no — don't. They're saying, "It's okay, use 'transmitter.'" I'm saying, "Tell me the word you want. I can get this!"

They might be using a Latin verb — like whatever "luminosity" would mean. I know it means bright, I know it means luminescent, but there's another way to interpret "luminous," which is like a transmitter.

VOICE: As we mentioned earlier, there are many wavelengths of energy which are not visible to your physical eyes and senses. Indeed, this goes beyond even your detectable forms of radiation and into subtler energies of what you'd call "spiritual matter." I personally refer to it as "astral matter."

For the higher you go, you realize that spirit has very little to do with any kind of form that can be separate from yourself. Rather "spirit" is a term used to describe is-ness. Being. That which has no name. That which permeates everything. That which has no break in its own continuity. That which is everywhere and beyond.

In you, in me, in the grass, in the molecules of air, even in the darkness. That is a level that is so high, you might even call it the endgame. For that is what we refer to as spirit.

But for the layman, thinking of ghosts and subtle astral realms, this is what they call spirit, of course. I don't refer to that as spirit — you will notice I commonly refer to it as "the astral." And there is a reason for that, but that is for a later discussion as well. Please continue.

JOHN: On that topic then, are we all — how should I phrase it — at different levels of existence? Are there different relationships between spirit and what would be called the "physical"? And does every level have its own version of physical? Meaning—

VOICE: Good question. We understand your question, but for the sake of the book, please clarify — continue when you said, "Meaning ..."

JOHN: So, physical means the common environment, shared by all the beings in that level, I suppose is how I would say it. Or not even just the common environment but, say, whatever form the body takes could be considered physical in that level. And then the things that are commonly perceived by the different beings at that level could be their version of physical. But it would have different properties from our version of physical.

VOICE: Physical at the level that you are talking about — we need to correct some terms — you are referring to "form." For there is only one physical dimension, which is the one that you appear to be in now. However, that being said, there are other dimensions that have form. That the form is not born, as it were, and nor does it die. Does this clarify your question at all?

JOHN: Yes — and I suppose that's just a matter of terminology — because to me I see physical as form, I guess to me it's the same thing, in a sense.

VOICE: Ah, but in the astral plane there still appears to be form for a time.

JOHN: Yes, and how would you define form in that way? Would you define form as anything that is perceived as external?

VOICE: Correct. Anything perceptually seen, anything that you perceive is something that is outside of you, apart from you, that has shape, that has substance. That is what we could say form is.

JOHN: And does form then, as you go to higher levels, play less and less of a role, in a sort of phased way, a phased-out way?

VOICE: That is exactly what it appears as for someone who is ascending. However, for those of us who have ascended, we realize that it was always formless, that we were merely having a dream, a dream that was governed by a mind that believed in separation, in objectification.

When you heal that belief, and you no longer need it, you take the blinders off and you begin to perceive reality as it truly is. Now that's not to say that at the level I encompass there isn't some form, but alas, I am a work in progress.

Now, we wish to address something. The information here does not seek to discredit or make the world of form seem like a bad or evil thing. This is not at all the case. In fact, if you are to take my words quite literally, there *is* nothing to get upset about. What we endeavour to do here is to help raise awareness to a greater reality; indeed, one could call it "home" — you've been using that term lately.

As I said, spirit, in its true form, is ever-present and permeating everything all at once. It is endless and has no divisions or breaks in its continuity, for that is your home, that is the state in which you belong. However, currently you are experiencing the complete opposite of that state.

You experience yourself as a separate tiny entity in a sea of other entities, each with his own desires, her own wishes, some of them friend, others foe, in a world where you're born and appear to die, where the days turn to night, where everyone appears unique and different. No matter where you look, it's always opposition, it's always separation.

This experience is one that your soul has chosen for a purpose. That purpose is to heal. This is a good time to mention that each and every being that appears to exist and is born into this universe is a part of a great mission — to be an apostle of peace and a courier of healing, for each and every one of you are great heroes in disguise sent on a mission, participating in the great universal healing.

Eventually, individually at first, there are beings that begin to awaken and no longer need to incarnate into physical form. This is not a new concept. And for the most part is a completely correct concept — the only mistake often made is those who believe that they are ready to ascend past incarnation. We often say, if you're truly enlightened, you'll be so happy you won't even care about being enlightened anymore.

There is a species, not far away, within your galaxy even, that for a time, approximately a thousand years, of Earth years, has inexplicably been unable to reproduce. It is an epidemic among their people. They can find no physical faults. This is a very advanced species of extraterrestrial — of course they themselves don't call themselves that.

Their society is literally becoming extinct. They are a spacefaring civilization; in fact, they have vessels, some of which are the size of your moon, that can travel the diameter of the galaxy. It is quite impressive.

Their entire species, collectively, has come to its enlightenment and is leaving the need for physical form altogether. Oftentimes, even in your world today, extremely advanced beings are incapable of reproduction. This is not to say that having children is a sign of a primitive soul; that's not true. There are advanced beings who had children. For instance, your master Jesus did have children. Three, as a matter of fact. His bloodline currently survives and lives on Earth to this day, although it is not important to point out who those people are.

But most advanced beings who are approaching enlightenment tend not to reproduce. This is a symbol of a lack of division in their mind, which is incapable of dividing itself because they are returning to wholeness. As we said, many things that occur in nature are direct mirrors of what's going on in higher reality.

In approximately six to eight hundred more years, the advanced alien civilization we spoke of will, by your definition, be extinct. But by our definition, it will have rejoined their true position as ascended teachers. And all of you, every cry in the night, every whisper, will be known to those teachers, and if you wish to call on them for help, they will be there in an instant.

Indeed, there are human beings who possess these abilities and who have ascended as well on your planet; most of whom you do not even know. For not every enlightened being attains fame or renown. Most enlightened beings tend to do great services and great acts for a civilization, on their final lifetime, but this is not a prerequisite. Just as we said most advanced beings no longer have children, that, too, is not an absolute rule of thumb. For whatever spirit guides you to do, you will do. The difference being, the more advanced you become, you only listen to spirit's direction and nothing else.

It seems I've gone off on a tangent. I apologize.

JOHN: Hm. It was a very interesting tangent.

Okay, well ... the bee video! That was amazing.

VOICE: Hm. Oh, it created a buzz amongst you, did it.

JOHN: *Ha ha.* It sure did.

VOICE: Forgive me my attempt at joining in your humour. I'm out of practice.

JOHN: What do you think of our humour?

VOICE: Well. We find it very amusing; of course, keep in mind we know you intimately, so we are on the inside.

JOHN: Yes.

VOICE: Humour is a gift. It is often a trait of an advanced being as well. It has been said on my side, I have never met an advanced being who wasn't smiling or couldn't laugh. One of the traits of a true teacher of spirit is one who inspires laughter.

One of the things we wish to point out is that, generally speaking, you and Brough never joke about suffering. Unless it's your own. We find that quite interesting. There are many people in your world who think they're funny, but they're not.

Brough has often said that sarcasm is the weakest form of humour; we find that quite clever. To have a good sense of humour is to have a sense of timing, rhythm, as well as to be in tune with the other people around you. There is a clever saying in your world: Laughter is a language spoken by all.

JOHN: Do you guys joke around, like, what form does humour take in your world? Is it the same?

VOICE: It's an excellent question. Of course, what two children might find funny differs only it its level of sophistication in comparison to what two college professors might find funny. However, no matter what the two entities are amused by, they both feel exactly the same.

Most recently, I found myself quite amused at watching the script of life unfold in several different directions. At the risk of sounding ... borderline cruel, Brough's moodiness has often been a topic of debate between the guides.

We of course are sympathetic; we realize that his moodiness is a complete side effect of being a psychic medium. Oftentimes indeed his moods aren't even his own. It's hard enough for some people to control their own moods — Brough has the job of ten men.

Much like watching a DVD movie in your world, where you can observe several different outcomes depending on which story you choose to go with, depending on which edit of the movie you choose to watch, I was able to unfold several different outcomes in Brough's life should he respond to a person in a certain manner versus another manner, and watching the drastic differences, depending on which mood Brough was in, was quite amusing to me. In fact you could call it hilarious. He is indeed a live wire.

JOHN: So, you can watch in that way, you can—

VOICE: Only as a means to help guide him down a preferred path for his well-being. You may think of it similar to being a soldier in a field of mines. Your guide is like a commanding officer speaking through a radio, warning you to take two steps forward and three steps to the right to avoid a landmine on your left. So that is what we do. It is one function of what we do.

JOHN: That's really entertaining … that…

[*I start to laugh.*]

VOICE: You have no idea.

[*My laughter is building.*]

VOICE: It may interest you that two of the scripts that could have played out would have resulted in the absolute permanent end of your friendship with Brough.

[*Our entity begins slipping into laughter in midsentence.*]

JOHN: Oh?

VOICE: Two of the seven scripts.

JOHN: So, did this involve me then?

VOICE: Not directly, no.

JOHN: Okay. But through some offshoot, ramification, somehow it might have ended up with us not being friends?

VOICE: Normally—

[*He goes into a full belly laugh and is having trouble getting the sentence out.*]

JOHN: Is that you laughing? Or Brough laughing ... or both?

VOICE: No, it's ... forgive me ... I just ... I'm just contemplating ... normally ... for human beings, the complete—

[*I go into a high-pitched hysterical laugh that I can't control.*]

—the complete devastation of a relationship comes about three or four times in a life!

[*I am doubled over and turned away. He continues in a high-pitched laughing voice, barely able to speak.*]

It's truly remarkable ... it's remarkable how often ... it is remarkable how often it is with this one. One can say, he's gifted!

[*We are both collapsed. Eventually they start speaking again, with the laughter still breaking through.*]

VOICE: You asked.

Before he was born, he absolutely made sure he would always have an exit. This was important to his soul's growth. Of course, we're laughing about this, but there is a realistic justification for this kind of a process.

You see, Brough's mission was so strictly laid out before him, there was no way he was going to be anything other than what he is. And so, in order for his soul to manifest some sense or semblance of freedom in life, he has to play that out in his relationship forms, so ... we laugh, of course, but it is, in his sense, his own certain exercise of free will. He always has power to walk away from a person, and that's a gift he has in this life.

Very similar to how some people can get jobs and change jobs at will, and their job doesn't really matter as much, Brough can do the same thing with relationships. We just find it funny because lately it has been a topic for us to do some repair work in his relationship zone. So you see, this was a source of great amusement.

Laron is not laughing, though, I should point out. I simply find it funny on my end of things.

JOHN: Now, I'm very curious that you had mentioned Alessia? Because we've been talking about Laron a lot, and I've been very interested to hear about Laron and her interest in me and my life and my psychology and so on, and then I'm sort of thinking, there was this "A" person, and I want to know more. I want to know more about that.

VOICE: Yes, your spiritual guide. We could call her a life guide, as Laron is a life guide to Brough. She was assigned to you at birth. Again, I say the word "assigned" — that denotes to you that there are some sort of agencies involved, but there aren't; her soul had chosen to be a guide and she had found herself magnetically drawn to you and psychically connected.

And to use the term "love" is an understatement. Total admiration, total love, total joy. There's a song that Laron had guided Brough to in his sixteenth year of life. And it was a song by an artist in your world known as Amanda Marshall. And the song is entitled "I Believe in You."

Brough was sitting in his family basement, watching the music video on the big-screen television, being emotionally moved by the song. The music video of course, if you take some time to watch it, shows Amanda Marshall standing and clapping and cheering on a young child as he moves through life, turns into a middle-aged man, and eventually becomes an old man. Amanda stays the same age.

Laron attracted Brough to this video to give him the concept of what a spiritual guide is. That was when Brough had a flash vision of an image of Laron in his mind, smiling and clapping for him. This image stuck with him for many years.

Then in his final year of high school, as you know, Laron was able to imprint that very image onto a roll of film, which now sits on his shelf in his office. That image, never being seen before except in his own mind, and that face, having been a familiar face appearing to him since he was a young child.

And so, we encourage you to watch that video, tonight perhaps, with Brough. Because that video encapsulates exactly what your spirit guide is and how she feels about you. Not everyone's guide is the opposite gender. You and Brough are just good with the gals, it seems.

Of course, as you ascend, the need for gender itself becomes totally obsolete. You'd be interested to know that through previous lifetimes you've been many genders.

JOHN: Hm. Yeah, I'm not surprised at that, actually.

VOICE: People often forget, and it is one of Brough's favourite sayings to point out that men have nipples too. Now the obvious comical value of that statement aside, it is true that in the womb all creatures are female. Men are simply inverted women. Gender itself one day will be seen as minor detail. Indeed, it should already be this way. And people shouldn't be stereotyped as much as they are.

One of the very powerful focuses of groups like ours, in the last three hundred years of your time on Earth, has been to fight for equality amongst people. If you read any of the classical literature of mediumship, oftentimes those mediums were fighting for women's equality and women's liberation in a day when women weren't even allowed to vote, much less hold down meaningful jobs and earn money.

We are happy that in this part of the world, at least, there is more equality nowadays, but this is not the case, this is not so in every part of your world, we must remind you of that. Now our personal interests are not specifically about those social issues but rather about assisting you in your own advancement and your own graduation into becoming spiritual teachers in this life.

We believe there will be a day where you, John, no longer have to sign in to an office and do a typical day job. Also, it's true: Brough will continuously, until the day that it is his time to make his transition, be doing readings. You have an opportunity to walk away from the conventional and move more into esoteric realms one day. To give too much information on that subject, however, would be a hinderance. For it is important that you, to some degree, find your own way.

As your guide well knows, it is within your psychological makeup currently that you feel as though you have come to your own conclusions. It's still a very important concept that you're psychologically attached to. As time goes on and you develop spiritually, you will lose the attachment to feeling as though you drew solid conclusions, and you will allow yourself to surrender more to guidance.

But we caution you not to rush that progress. Although it is true that that would be a measure of progress for you, there is no rush. You must be gentle and go at the pace that you can handle. And for now, do not quit your day job.

JOHN: Well, gotta pay the bills.

VOICE: Mm.

JOHN: But yes of course, I'd be very open to doing other things.

When you say conclusions, do you mean a decision that I feel I have made solely myself, a decision to do something? Is that what you mean in terms of a conclusion?

VOICE: Correct.

As I alluded to earlier, the more advanced you become, you only listen to spirit. If you were to be snapped into that state of being, it would be very disturbing to your current psychological makeup. That's why we usher you or we encourage you to go slow.

JOHN: Well, and I think I already went through a period where I went to the other end of the spectrum in terms of handing it completely over to spirit, or at least I felt I was, when I was younger, and I think I lost too much traction in my life, and maybe I'm reacting to that a little bit still.

VOICE: Yes, it is true, there are periods of clarity and awakening that occur, and oftentimes during those periods, it becomes painfully apparent that other faculties need development as well before you can fully make the leap.

For instance, much to the point of what you were just making, for the clarity of the readers, there are those who believe that to be truly spiritual you must give up attachment to all material things. Now this is a very true concept and it is the hallmark of advancement.

But just to clarify, giving up material things does not mean throwing your children into volcanoes, nor does it mean to cease eating food, nor does it mean to strip yourself naked.

Giving up attachment, psychological attachment, giving up the ideas you have about the physical, is all that is required. You don't have to actually give up the material; you're going to have to do that anyway. It's about giving up the importance that you put on it.

Which, of course, allows the ego to step aside long enough for spirit to then tell you what to use things for. So, many people have the giving up, the surrender part, down pat. But what they fail to do is develop the necessary clairaudience to hear spirit guiding them from there. And so, they get one part wrong and the other part right.

As you develop your clairaudience and your other spiritual faculties, you'll be able to give up attachment to things while still using them with complete wisdom and fluidity. In fact you'll find that your ideas will be clear and laser-beam sharp. And they will always yield positive results. And that consistency will yield trust for spirit, and you will begin to start to depend more and more on spiritual guidance.

And this is indeed getting ahead of ourselves. Did I answer your question?

JOHN: Yeah, I think you did ... I usually have to go back over what's been said a couple times to really absorb it. I find that's what's happening, that it's not until I transcribe it and read it. And it's partly because, while we're talking, I have so many different offshoots of thought and I start thinking back to things that were said earlier. So I'm not able to fully absorb it at the time.

VOICE: Don't pressure yourself. Brough is in the same boat as you; he is not thinking or analyzing anything; the words are coming through free-association speech. He is becoming more relaxed and allowing me to speak through him. Whereas his fears that he would have nothing interesting to say earlier did indeed get in the way somewhat.

Again, it's another symbol of him allowing his ego to step aside. When you stop caring about whether what you're saying is interesting, oftentimes that's when you say the most interesting things. As that saying goes, "Stop trying to have fun, just have fun trying."

For the sake of clarity, although the interaction between us is that of pupils with a higher being, your spirit guides are involved, but they are not the principal identities behind these channellings. Both Laron and Alessia are there and they are supportive.

And if you wish, we can arrange to have communication with them. I cannot guarantee that Brough will be able to channel them in this same fashion; perhaps Brough will be able to create some kind of a psychical link, similar to when he does a reading.

But even in his readings, he is able to give objective messages, but sentences from the speaker are not exactly how they come through. For example, in a reading with Brough, he may say, "Your father is giving me the name Garrett." And Brough receives that message through an image of the name Garrett in his mind.

The client may then say, "Yes, that was my father's name." So you see, when Brough is doing a reading, he's not channelling the entity in the first person, he's speaking about it in the third. That same effect would occur with your spirit guides.

Having said that, they are here with me and with you, and I can translate information for them, relay it to you. Perhaps if Brough were to develop someday into a full-trance medium, his guide could come through him, and yours as well.

JOHN: Yeah, this concept of a guide — I think I always had some sense of a team, or a person, being involved. I mean, I've always spoken to whoever's out there, but I'd never identified it as a person, a specific person.

Although with the EVPs and so on, I did start to do that, and I had this idea of "Penelope," and Brough and I were wondering earlier where that actual name came from — Brough said it came from him. And that may just be another name for Alessia. But that's the first time I started to think of an actual person, an individual.

VOICE: Yes, the Penny dropped.

JOHN: *Ha ha* — good! That's very good. Then of course, Brough introduced me to this — I mean, I'd heard of spirit guides and so on, but he had this actual photo! And had a person he identified by name.

VOICE: That's right. Indeed, he did not even recall the circumstances, the exact circumstances as to when he saw that image appear in his mind telepathically before it appeared on the photo, but tonight I had reminded him, through Laron's assistance, that it happened when she guided him to that specific music video.

JOHN: And, I feel there's things from my childhood that lie under the surface, things that happened, I feel it's around the age of five or six or something.

VOICE: Hm.

JOHN: And, I wonder if it's to do with my guide. I feel that I experienced something directly, and uh … it's there, and—

VOICE: Stand by. Your spirit guide is speaking to me.

That was in a house — did you have a move of home around the age of six?

JOHN: I certainly did. Precisely at that age.

[*Brough knows that I grew up in Oakville; he has no idea of the details of when I moved or that I had moved houses at all.*]

VOICE: The home before that had a spirit that required displacement, a ghost as you'd call it, and your spirit guide was extremely active in your third, fourth, and fifth year in protecting you from the interference of that, of that spirit woman.

There was a swinging door off the kitchen that would routinely move by itself.

[*This is a shock because I remember that our kitchen did have a swinging saloon-style door, but I haven't thought of it since long before meeting Brough. This is the kind of detail that only lives in my distant memory and would be almost impossible for Brough to know about.*]

Your spirit guide was attempting to prevent your childhood self from receiving trauma from the spirit world, which would have thus caused you to go into a deep denial about spirit for the rest of your life. So she was very active in your life during those years.

So suffice to say, you had spiritual activities at a very early age. You could say it was even in your formative years. But you did feel that.

JOHN: Yeah. And I feel my sister is involved in that somehow. I don't know if it's that same situation or a different situation.

VOICE: Yes, it was the same situation but a different entity associated with the old lady. A man who had committed suicide earlier in her life was also a frequent visitor. Your sister would dream of a car pulling up outside her window, that would be the man coming home. This disturbed individual would be frightening to her and she would have nightmares about it.

Indeed, your spirit guides were working steadfast to protect you from these entities at that tender age.

JOHN: And there's a song that both she and I have some memory associated with. And she won't even listen to that song.

VOICE: The reason why that song in particular affects you was not because the song itself was played by any entity, but that song was popular in that era, and the single phrase from it had stricken both of you due to an experience when you had seen a blinding light coming through a doorway, which was the beginnings of an interaction of spirit.

[At the mention of a blinding light, I gasp. I mentioned the song maybe once or twice to Brough, probably when we first met, about ten years earlier. It's possible that this information is coming from Brough's memory, but it's something we never talked about since then, and I feel that even if he remembers there was a song, he won't remember the name of it.

In 1976, when I was five years old, Manfred Mann's Earth Band released the song "Blinded by the Light," originally by Bruce Springsteen. The lyrics are not about anything in particular, mostly wordplay Springsteen wrote using a rhyming dictionary. The song has always been eerie to me and my sister, with its opening staccato keyboards and choral background vocals. She simply refuses to listen to it. It came on the car radio once as adults and she shut the radio off.]

Unfortunately, we spirit guides cannot always be everywhere and cannot always protect you from every single instance when it comes to lower-level entities. However, the more advanced beings there are involved, the more you are protected.

It was indeed a doorway opening — that was an attempt to bring the entities who were earthbound over to the other side, to reunite them with their families. As small children, you were witness to this event and naturally repressed it, as it was frightening to you. And later on, through psychology, when hearing that song, "Blinded by the Light," you were able to associate it to a traumatic event that had been repressed in your minds.

This was called a displacement. That's what we call it when we work to remove or help a spirit let go of its psychological attachment to the Earth realm.

Does this make sense to you?

JOHN: It really does ... well I mean, I had no idea of that interpretation of what had happened.

VOICE: You were more well-protected — your sister definitely had more close encounters, if you will ... both for the sake that she is very sensitive to this realm, but also because, for some reason, her spirit guide was less aware of the problem.

[I just used the term "close encounters" with Brough that day. I texted him "close encounters of the turd kind," for no particular reason other than that I was thinking of watching the movie, Close Encounters of the Third Kind, *again. I associated the movie with feelings similar to those brought up by "Blinded by the Light." The song and the movie were released within a year of each other, and so the movie may also have become associated with these events in my mind. An iconic image from the movie, of a boy standing before a door filled with bright light emitted by UFOs, mirrors the event described above.*

There is a photo of my brother and sister and I in that house, by the Christmas tree. I look freaked out by something. My brother is crawling on the floor. Next to him, there is a streak of light coming from the bottom of the photo. Around the light is a kind of haze that extends to the top of the photo. When I tried adjusting the saturation and contrast to bring out the shape of the haze, it took on a human-like form, with a face looking in the direction of me and my sister.]

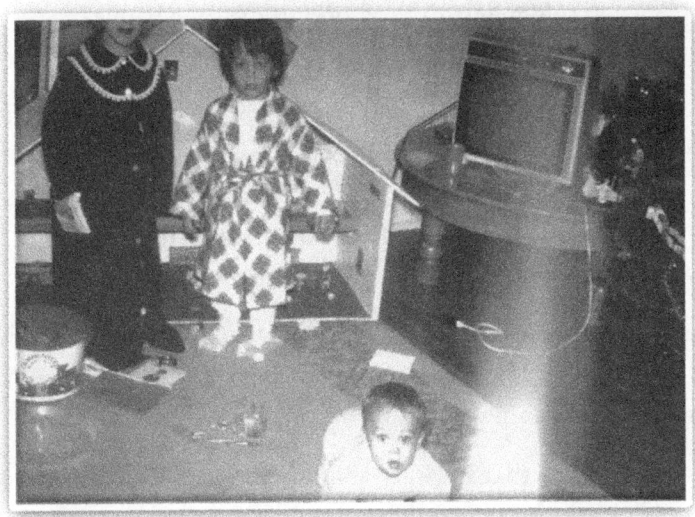

John (centre) with his sister and brother in their childhood home in Oakville, Ontario. A streak of light with surrounding haze appears on the right side.

I'm sorry, finish what you were saying.

JOHN: I'm just — astounded at everything you're saying. I mean, you're, you knew the exact song. I guess I shouldn't be surprised at these things, but ... I'm absolutely floored.

And this happened at the first house then, before the move?

VOICE: That's correct. The trauma happened at the first house. You psychologically became attached to the song after you'd moved.

JOHN: It's funny because I was going to talk to Brough — that house came into my mind tonight, and I was going to talk to him about it. I kept wanting to bring it up 'cause it had these secret passages up in the attic, that I loved.

VOICE: Yes exactly. That house — the male energy had shot himself, not necessarily on the property — the one who was more tormentful to your sister. She may have some deeply repressed memories of hearing a car pull up, then seeing a man walk into the front door and come upstairs.

JOHN: She has told me that she associates the song with a car on the side of a road or something like that.

VOICE: Correct. He had killed himself and then his spirit continually drives home as if after a workday. The older woman is the one that Alessia was protecting you from specifically. She was a bitter old woman. It is beyond my current frame of reference to tell whether the man was her husband from years bygone or a son of hers.

I believe her husband was the one who killed himself and her son was estranged from her. She died alone in the house some years later. And she took a particular interest in you.

It's useful to know that we were able to displace those spirits, your spirit guide has informed me. They are no longer earthbound.

JOHN: And a few years ago I went to Oakville to walk around and I met an older woman who lived across the street from that house, and I was just walking by her and she was on her porch, and she invited me in and we sat on her porch and talked about that neighbourhood and the house and just the different people who had lived there before.

It was always my favourite house, and it's funny because I never wanted us to leave there, and I remember driving away from it and being in the back of a pickup and being really sad that we were leaving that house. And that's always a refrain with my mom, that I'm still mad at them for moving out of there.

So it surprises me in that way, to hear that there were these types of things associated with it.

VOICE: Ah, but why? Your soul on some level knew that you were to be a psychic technician. The popular movie in your world, *Ghostbusters*, depicts scientists who run towards phenomena, not away from it.

JOHN: Yes! Yeah. So there was a part of me attracted to it.

VOICE: Oh, very much so. It would interest you to know that, usually, earthbound entities do take refuge in unattended areas of homes, often attic spaces and basements and crawl spaces. This isn't because they're attempting to be creepy, it is because spirit entities become very fatigued very quickly.

They're only able to make a short burst outside of their slumber-like state. When you're asleep at night, you're often unaware that you're dreaming. Many hours could pass, and when you wake up it only feels like you were asleep for moments or minutes.

The same can occur to spirits who are earthbound; while years of Earth time can go by, they were merely experiencing moments — isolated incidents of being awake. Naturally their soul, or their ethereal body, or astral body, will go back to an area of the home that is least disturbed, that is most quiet for them to slumber. Those crawl spaces contained the old lady, who took special interest in you.

JOHN: The spaces up in the attic?

VOICE: Correct. Oftentimes you would be crawling through and bringing plastic soldiers with you and toys, and unbeknownst to you, an old woman on her hands and knees would be staring at you from down a crawl space.

You would feel her presence and be strangely compelled by it. Which would only disturb her more.

JOHN: It would disturb her that I was compelled by it?

VOICE: Correct — you were in her space, you see, disturbing her sleep.

JOHN: Hm. Why was she interested in me?

VOICE: Her son had been estranged from her. You represented, on a psychological level, a son figure that she had lost. Oftentimes entities who are earthbound will latch onto or take special interest in a being on Earth that reminds them of someone from their past life. This happens largely at a subconscious level.

Much like this morning, when Brough left his body and was greeted by ancestors of his in the spirit world. Much like a ghost, he himself projected his own family from his Earth life onto those spirit beings.

JOHN: So those beings that he saw were not his ancestors, they were just other people?

VOICE: They were indeed his ancestors, but what I mean to say is, he referred to them as his sisters on Earth, his cousin. In that state, when you are still too psychologically attached to Earth, it becomes difficult for you to see clearly.

Indeed, you hallucinate your own past life on top of the current existence. That's why ghosts are often confused and unaware that they are dead.

But this ties back to the very law that I have been discussing with you since the beginning of these channellings, does it not? The more you become aware of yourselves, the more of reality you become able to see and perceive. In a sense, you are all ghosts on a journey of awakening.

JOHN: So a picture can be blurry or it can go into high definition, depending on your perception.

VOICE: Those are the best cases. A person can also be looking at something and hallucinating a totally different picture over top of it, much like a schizophrenic in your world. And believe it or not, that passes for normal human relationship. For how many of you date someone and hallucinate your mother or your father over top that person?

What I pose is that once you heal all the fractures in your mind, you will finally, for the first time, start to see people as they truly are. And what you will find will never cease to amaze you and bring you closer to joy.

We wish to take this opportunity to point out that earthbound spirits are a rare condition and always a temporary one. No one is bound to be a ghost forever.

And you do not have to be a bad person to become a ghost. Indeed, the more we progress with these channellings and the more you get to know the material that I am presenting, the more you will realize that you are no different than ghosts, that all existence is a game of taking off the blinders, as it were, learning to heal the fractures in the mind.

And as you do, you begin to ascend and ascend, like a child coming out of a daze, out of a sleep, or a patient rising out of a coma; you begin to rejoin the ranks, as it were, of the real, awakened world.

There are many people in your world who believe that a great awakening is coming here. Now this is a preposterous concept. It is about as preposterous as those who believe that the master Jesus is going to return in physical form.

The truth is that to awake in a dream is an oxymoron. To slowly awaken means that you release the psychological attachment to dreams. And as you do that, in your incarnation, you will begin to exhibit advanced mental powers.

These powers will make you look like a mystic. Some people would call people saints who have these powers. Others will call them miracle workers. And these symbols or effects are no more than the vision of a mind that has begun to realize it is dreaming and can now control the dream.

Until such a day comes, when it is time to awaken and you gently lay your body aside, without pain and suffering, and ascend into a higher realm — beyond even the astral realms of distraction, all the way into that inviting light at the end of all the stars, the edge of the known universe, much like a pinprick where a stream of sunlight shines through the fabric of time and space, which are themselves simple illusions that were created by your soul — you suddenly realize that you were never in danger, that you never left home, that all those lifetimes of pain and disease and suffering and separation and death were just a bad dream.

And that everyone you ever loved and ever will love, indeed the people that you had great lessons with, both positive and negative, are all there and part of your current existence. They were never apart from you. And on that day, you will rejoice and remember the great forgotten song of home. And all of this will seem like a silly fantasy, like a war game a child once played with itself. And each of you is on a steadfast course to that awakening.

And it is important now to mention that there is a difference between the types of information we are channelling and what John so affectionately refers to as "New Agey bullcrap." Now the New Age are still immature souls who are attempting to make this material world important — who are trying to, as Brough has said, spiritualize matter. We can't bring the real world into a dream, for it is universal law that you surrender your dreams to reality, not the other way around.

As we said earlier, it is not our mandate that you surrender and give up anything physical. Rather that you simply change your mind about it; give up your psychological attachment to it. For just as a ghost must eventually leave a house or an object or a person that it is psychologically attached to, that house or that person or that being, it appears, will continue to exist for a time, and always a finite time, in this dreamworld of yours.

For eventually everything returns to dust. Everything here is fluid, whereas that entity has rejoined with itself and its loved ones in a higher form, in a higher plane, in its truer form, you could say, and they've come home.

Does this inspire further questions?

JOHN: You've mentioned once or twice the idea that you on your side learn from us as we go through our experiences, and that to me was quite a radical idea, the fact that you could learn from us. Could you explain a bit about that — how do you learn from us?

VOICE: Mm-hm, of course.

The higher you go, much like climbing the peak of a mountain, you can take a moment and look around and see more. Indeed, when you begin to climb a mountain, when you are at the foot, you can look up all the way to the peak. And if you should have a friend that is already at the top looking down, their vantage point can show you much more about your existence. They can tell you to take this trail instead of that trail and avoid certain obstacles.

Alas, we are still on the same mountain, you and I. I am simply further ahead. And as I help guide you up the trail, perhaps assisting you at certain pitfalls that I had overcome, not only am I reminded of certain lessons of my own, but I also learn a deeper form of compassion as I assist you and use my abilities to engineer situations and patterns in your life. I am putting into practice the use of advanced mental abilities, which are preparing me for further work at higher realms yet, of existence.

You see, with more power comes more responsibility. Before all of us rejoin the ranks as ascended masters, where every single whisper, every single prayer, every single person is intimately woven into the fabric of our awareness, we must start small, on a case-by-case basis.

You see, it may surprise you and perhaps turn some of you off to know that you are all on the path to becoming god-like creatures. The term "creature" is not even correct. For formlessness has no creaturehood.

So each and every one of us is on the path to become a master; there is nothing else to become. But thinking of it symbolically, the master is simply an awakened mind, one that is rejoined with reality, where there is nothing without it. So, as you begin to awaken and achieve more abilities, you are given tasks to help other beings along their journey; to carry your brother as it were, to help lighten the load.

And that allows you to practise your abilities, which will help prepare you to fully let go of form and rejoin with your own soul's totality one day. Most people who hear this will find it a distasteful idea. For they have no concept of anything beyond form.

But with future material that is intended to come through, as well as practices that we give you, the idea of non-corporeal reality will slowly become not only clear to you but absolutely palatable. In fact it is your natural state. The life that you live currently is nothing but a costume that you put on to hide from your own greatness.

Thus slowly and surely, take off the costume, starting with the gloves and working your way through until all that is left is your eternal self. And along the way, jewels, precious spiritual gifts, will be bestowed to you. And levels of joy, which you have previously never known, will occur.

And as you heal your mind, states of being, which you have been afflicted with and thought would never leave you — such as loneliness, despair, isolation, feelings of malaise — will simply vanish without any attention to them whatsoever. You will simply no longer have those sufferings.

And these are all side effects of you regaining your inheritance as spirit. All of which can be and will be accomplished while you're still in a body. You do not need to die to accomplish this.

However, even when you're free of a body, and like myself, have very little need for a new one, except to communicate messages to those who are willing to listen, you can still continue to grow, through extending yourself and bringing love and healing to all levels of the universe.

And we all have a part to play in the great universal healing. You and I and all those who you know intimately and will know in this life are part of a family, as it were. A soul cluster. Much like a system of stars hanging loosely in the night sky, we neighbour each other. Together, we shine light and point the way to the end of time and beyond.

The connection grows thin, but we wish for you to end the session tonight with any other thoughts that you may have. Would you like to share?

JOHN: I don't know. I'm just really blown away by everything tonight. I mean the energy of the session and the fact that we went so long, and it was able to be so sustained, it was amazing. And the stuff about me, of course, is a lot for me to process and perhaps talk to my sister about sometime, if I feel the time's right.

VOICE: It was our intention tonight to provide you with, as you'd call it, an epic ending to the first chapter. I think that it is fair to say that this segues into you being able to tell the story in an eloquent way, but a detailed way, of your childhood leading up to this channelling, so that they could understand the references that were made and why they were personal to you.

But we definitely want to suggest that you do not concern yourself with the order in which you post these channellings in your book, as Brough had conveyed to you from us. Because of the nature of how Brough can access this information, how the limitation exists, that we can only tell you what you're ready to hear — even if we wish to tell you more, you will only be able to hear what you are ready to hear. Which explains, by the way, why we want you to practise spiritual advancement — because it of course will open the channel even further for us to give you even more information.

You must categorize this information and put it in a more palatable context for the reader. Not everyone is as advanced as you, we must remind you. And indeed, this same concept extends into the audio of our recordings. Brough's hesitance does extend from us, only because we are aware that you are advanced enough to understand the context of what's being given, as well as to differentiate between the pure messages and some of the filtering techniques that are used through the medium, among many other subtleties that a layman would not be able to discern.

We have chosen you partially because you are good translators. Bear that in mind. We do trust your ability to polish the material before you release it, similar to polishing gemstones. And a good jeweller will polish and shape a gemstone and then lay it in a beautiful ring before presenting it, for its maximum beauty and its maximum impact. You must do the same with this material; with our guidance of course.

[Authors' note: Our approach to editing the text of these dialogues is to make only minor changes to correct any grammatical or structural issues that may get in the way of comprehension or narrative flow. Some phrasing may be effective in spoken word but needs adjustment for the written format. We do not generally indicate that a change has been made using square brackets or ellipses, so as to not interrupt the flow of the text and distract the reader. Here are some examples of edits we have made: Just above, the word "hesistance" was originally said as "hesitancy."

In the next paragraph, starting with "We wish you good night," "sincerity and positivity" was spoken as "sincerity, positivity." When listing a series of terms, the Voice will often omit "and," which works well when delivered but needs the addition when written.

Italics were not specified by the Voice. We add them to indicate that something was emphasized vocally, or to clarify meaning. In a very few cases, we rearranged sentence or paragraph structure for clarity. If there is a significant change to meaning, such as the earlier case where "ephemeral" was replaced by "ineffable," a note is made to the reader. I would estimate that over 95% of the channelled material is written exactly as it was spoken.

In the audio that will be released from the chanelling sessions, the reader will be able to experience the original delivery. We didn't record any sessions from this book on video, but that is something we will consider doing in the future.]

We wish you good night and wish for you to remember that we convey these messages with sincerity and positivity, and that you are indeed loved by many at all levels. If you could know the depth of feeling and regard that you engender from us, the very notion of feeling alone or isolated would make you giggle.

And fear not, boys, for as you learn to awaken your own psychic abilities — when I say "psychic abilities" I'm referring to something far more than the diagnostic tools that you're used to — but as I alluded to earlier, when you become better transmitters and are able to play with the dream of life a little more actively, always with the guidance of spirit, mind you, you will literally be able to wish new friends into existence. You simply call forth whomever you desire, and within hours, days, sometimes even minutes, they will appear.

And with that gift will come the responsibility of having to repair old relationships that you thought were forgotten, lost. For you cannot have it one way without having it the other. If you are to call in new people, you must also heal the old. For everything is a reflection of the other.

Until next time.

BROUGH: Ah, I think we can scrap that one; it sounded like crap. Clearly, I can't do this sober.

JOHN: *Ha ha ha.*

BROUGH: That was me partly, laughing during that laughing part. Because I can hear the cadence more than I can translate it, and his voice was just like, "It's re*mar*kable! It's almost impressive! I mean usually a typical human has maybe three opportunities to completely decimate a friendship, but on a consistent basis, Brough is capable of annihilating and alienating everyone from his life."

[*Both laughing.*]

This is what he was laughing to hell about. This is what he found amusing. I have the capacity to become a complete misanthrope. That was an interesting analysis. I had never thought of it like that before. That my mission as a psychic is so set in stone that *my* own version of free will is to be able to say "fuck off" to people. What are you thinking?

JOHN: I'm just completely stimulated. All that stuff about my childhood — do you remember that?

BROUGH: Vaguely. Ghosts. And the old lady. I could see her; she was gaunt in the face.

JOHN: I'm completely vibrating right now. I mean, it's unearthing stuff from when I was four or five. They knew the exact song. And I've told you about that song but it was, like, ten years ago and you probably didn't remember that.

BROUGH: I don't remember it.

JOHN: You didn't just suddenly pull that out of your memory banks; that was them. They told me the exact song. I didn't give them any prompting, other than that there was a song. I'm just amazed. I felt like it all opened up even further tonight.

BROUGH: Yeah. Way to make up for some lost time.

JOHN: The things they were saying about the house.

BROUGH: What about the house?

JOHN: Well, they were saying I moved when I was six, which I did. You didn't know that. I knew there was something back there, that my sister and I were —her more so — both freaked out about. And the song triggered that. The song was our memory of that, our signpost for that.

BROUGH: So what did they say tonight about the song?

JOHN: They said the song, which was called "Blinded by the Light" — you know the one by Manfred Mann?

BROUGH: Oh yeah, yeah, yeah.

JOHN: So that came out mid-'70s. It was right around that time. We would have moved out of that house in 1977. So basically there was a woman in the house and there was a man who had committed suicide.

BROUGH: Right, but how did the song apply to that?

JOHN: There was something about a doorway that opened up and a light that came through, and it was about getting spirits to move on.

BROUGH: And you saw that.

JOHN: And that's what we associated with that song.

BROUGH: So when you and your sister were just sort of playing and the song came on in the car or whatever.

JOHN: Well, I always thought that the song was playing at the time that something happened. But they said no it wasn't that, it was that it was a popular song at the time, and then maybe we heard it soon after and grafted that experience with the light onto the song.

And the whole laughing thing. I was actually laughing with them. Like, they emerged more in terms of being a person I can interact with.

BROUGH: He doesn't hold back. Like, if you want to know something, he'll tell you. "What do you find funny?" you ask. I could see it as he was explaining it. I could see like a script, like a whole wall of film and the different branches of that film, like all the different ways things would screw up. It was like little flaggles. That's my life just flying off the handle. And he's just laughing; he thinks it's just the most amusing thing!

[*Both laughing again.*]

BROUGH: Like as if the film breaks on the projector reel, it's just spinning and flailing! And my life is derailing. That was the answer to your question, what did he think was funny!

JOHN: This guy right here! It's like the funniest *Three Stooges* movie you've ever seen.

BROUGH: In one being. And it all hinges not on war, not on a murderer in a park, not on any of the normal dangers in life. It's on his *moods*. That's what was funniest to him. It was that moods alone have the power.

JOHN: To create all these potential realities.

BROUGH: Based on a state of mind. Which speaks a lot to what they're teaching, but also, being psychic, that's part of the heavy weight that you carry.

JOHN: It's stuff I've thought about before, that your different temperaments — it has to affect things.

BROUGH: And it's not an excuse; in fact, it makes me have to be that much more responsible all the time.

JOHN: Yeah. And I factor that in … in my…

BROUGH: Dealings with me!

JOHN: Yeah.

[*Both laughing.*]

BROUGH: He finds it very funny. This being has obviously mastered those types of things, like moods and stuff, I guess. I don't think spirit beings have that many moods anyway, but he seems advanced. Like I'm getting the impression that he is above the normal range of spirit guides or astral entities, that's for sure. He's not just a dead guy, like William, who comes through David Thompson.

JOHN: Well, it seems like there's Laron and Alicia, and there's him on a different level. That's what he was saying.

BROUGH: He does not seem like he wants to give an identity, because he doesn't necessarily associate himself with an identity. I was wanting to get his name, but he was like, "Don't worry, I don't go by that, it's not necessary. I don't identify like that."

JOHN: Yeah. And I think it's okay if we just leave it as that, but…

BROUGH: We could just end up calling it "the entity."

JOHN: I don't know if, for practical reasons, we would need a name.

BROUGH: But I think for the story itself, it's interesting, if we say that it doesn't want to be named.

JOHN: He Who Shall Remain Nameless.

BROUGH: The Artist Formerly Known As…

JOHN: I was just going to say that! We're doing a lot of that. Telepathy. Like they said, we'll argue with each other in our heads — at the same time!

BROUGH: Oh yeah. Both being correct about what the other would say. Which is an opportunity, through advanced abilities, to resolve conflict before one even exists. Which is akin to seeing the option lines.

JOHN: So, what we're doing actually has a value then, arguing with each other in our heads?

BROUGH: Doing it in our heads is akin to looking at the possible timelines and not going down them. 'Cause that's what they said to me today — I don't know why I'm so hell-bent on this audio thing! And I kind of knew it was them, psychically in me. But it was being overlaid on me with such urgency, like I couldn't sleep because of it.

And I had a voice in me saying, "JT is not going to do anything that you don't want to do, and he's not out to hurt you. He loves you." And then that calmed me down — but by the time that happened, I had already sent the emails, so I couldn't get there quick enough this time. But next time, little things like that, I'll try and tell you.

JOHN: Well, I used to get all, "What the fuck? Why is he getting so bossy about this?" But I'm learning more how to tell when you're latching psychically onto something, and I'm learning to roll with that.

BROUGH: But I think there's going to be equilibrium where I'll do less of that. Just as you're taking that less seriously, I'll be doing less of it, and it'll just disappear. There'll be harmony. Plus, you'll be hearing *them* more.

JOHN: I was thinking that. I think I already do.

BROUGH: Because the funny thing is, we both agree — all the material should be out in the public. It's just we have to format it properly.

One other thing I didn't verbalize is — we're very much working with this one entity. But our guides are present. But our guides and him — or it — weren't part of some conglomerate or some organized thing before. It's like he was definitely a principality. Our guides are with *us*. They're, like, standing beside us going, "Oh, hey!"

[*Reading this later on, Brough was unsure why he used the term "principality" as he is not familiar with it. One of the meanings according to* Merriam-Webster *is "an order of angels" in the Christian "celestial hierarchy." In this hierarchy, there are nine ranks of angels, with principality being third, after angel and archangel.*]

JOHN: Right, I see! As opposed to an alignment that formed with them first. So, he tuned in to us. He found us. So, he must have been aware of us from birth or whatever.

BROUGH: Part of his mental abilities are what allow the synchronicities to happen. That's the extent of manipulation of the space-time continuum he's able to perform. He's a very powerful entity. And he said that we ourselves — and I think he means all beings, but I also think *us* as well — have the potential to access powers of the mind that can affect reality the way that he can. That he's not even at the top.

JOHN: Wait, what do you mean by "he's not at the top"?

BROUGH: He said he's not going to pretend to be some kind of ascended master. He's no St. Germaine.

[*We imitate a channeller Brough found on YouTube called "St. Germaine" who speaks in a very unusual nasal voice. She makes a pun about "lay awake plan" vs. "layaway" plan.*]

JOHN: Lay awake plan — that was pretty good, actually. Actually, regarding puns, it's funny, in our session he made the pun about "creating quite a buzz" with the bee video.

BROUGH: Oh yeah, he's trying to be funny now.

JOHN: It was kind of a lame pun, but it was amusing anyway.

BROUGH: I don't think the bee rescuing the other bee was planned out by spirit. I think the bees were tapping into love. Love is spirit but it's not a controlling factor, it's a frequency. Any being that's tuned in to love will act in accordance with certain principles. It'll behave in a certain loving way.

JOHN: So even little bees could tap into that.

BROUGH: Yeah, everything is capable of love. It's taking love outside of the human framework, into a higher scope.

JOHN: It's inherent in nature.

BROUGH: This being says that it loves us but it doesn't have a physical body so it's not hormonal love, it's not sexy lust. It's very loving, it's a very loving force. My voice doesn't sound like its voice.

JOHN: Your voice goes a bit lower and it's very steady.

BROUGH: I can hear its voice and it's very smooth and very calming. And it's got a hint of joy in it. Which I can't convey, because in the trance state everything is just sedate.

JOHN: So there's more expression in the voice than what you're giving it?

BROUGH: Oh yeah. It's got a joyful jubilance to it. It's got a joyfulness to it. It's a happy voice. It's definitely masculine. Now I don't know if the masculinity is because it's coming through *me*, to some degree. But I don't get a sense of femininity. Like, our guides are both women and I very much sense them. But it also may have less attachment to gender.

JOHN: Well, that's what I was going to say — at that level, it's probably all hybrid, it's whole. It may manifest as more one or the other, for whatever reason.

BROUGH: It might not even be *human*.

JOHN: Well, I think you have to define "human" at that point.

BROUGH: Its last incarnation may have been on another terrestrial body, even another planet.

JOHN: If you have different incarnations on different planets, what does the concept of "human" even mean, in the other levels? Is human just one manifestation of individual consciousness? Does human mean specifically from Earth?

Cohesive Thinking

The W5 show aired about a week after our epic session. Brough and I watched it at my place. It started with a radio announcer–type voice booming, "Tarot cards, crystal balls, and psychic readings." Then it cut to Brough sitting with Dr. Smith, saying, "I'm going to close my eyes, tell you everything I see." Then the announcer: "The fantastic claims! The dire warnings!"

Anchorman Lloyd Robertson chimed in with, "This week we go undercover and enter the world of fortune tellers, who are really fortune takers. It appears one thing they can see coming clearly is their victims." They introduced Dr. Smith and explained that he believes psychic ability is real, in part because of "this man — Toronto psychic Brough Perkins." They cut to the reading from the apartment, the camera zooming in on Brough as he whispers, "George ... George."

BROUGH: There's a "G" name: George. Do you have a connection to a George?

CHRISTIAN: Yes.

BROUGH: Is that "Granddad" to you?

CHRISTIAN: Yes.

BROUGH: Okay. Please let me tell you, your grandfather, George, is watching over you. He's very proud of you.

The host Sandie Rinaldo asked Dr. Smith if he thought that Brough possessed psychic ability, to which he answered, "I think he does. He definitely does have an ability to pick up things that are not publicly available."

For the rest of the segment, they focused on fraudulent psychics that try to dupe people into spending huge amounts of money. Their reporters went into readings with a hidden camera, in one case capturing a woman telling the client, "You have a darkness around you" and that it would cost him $1,200 to have the darkness removed.

The purpose of the segment was not to explore psychic ability but to investigate fraud. They asked the question, "Is psychic ability real?" but didn't do the necessary digging. They showed Brough getting his grandfather George's name but left out his getting his great-aunt Dotty's name and relation, and other bits of information that Dr. Smith confirmed as correct.

The show included the usual claim of there being no empirical evidence for psychic ability, which isn't true, as there is a large body of controlled experiments that show strongly that psychic ability is measurable and real, as documented by researchers like Dean Radin. The problem is that people hear this claim that there is no evidence and repeat it and don't actually do the research to find out if it is true.

All in all, it was good to have Brough represent the non-fraudulent side of the business, even if the reality of his abilities was only left open as a hazy possibility.

The next day, on Sunday, March 20, we attempted channelling at 8:00 a.m. I'd been waking up almost every morning at 4:00 or 4:30 a.m. for a couple weeks, and it felt like it was due to an external force that was very eager for me to work on the project, as opposed to being my own sleep cycles or insomnia. Sometimes I would use the time to do project work, but it made it hard for me to function at my job and as a parent. I knew it wasn't sustainable.

BROUGH: I'm not sensing anything.

Oh, Laron's telling me they're not going to do that today. The entity has another plan.

She said, "Excellent work, excellent work. It's coming along really well, better than expected." What do you think of the whole news thing, Laron?

Oh, okay. Laron says that she thinks they treated *me* fairly with the news piece. It wasn't overly generous with the time that they gave to me or representative of the reading I gave, because the reading on Dr. Smith was far more detailed than just "your grandfather, George, says he's proud of you."

She said this will lead to bigger things. And I have to represent integrity. The integrity of the work. Or she's saying that I have to remember that putting integrity first is paramount. Because her impression to me is that this field of work isn't what it used to be — it used to be even better than it is now, in a sense.

In the Victorian era and the early psychical-research era, there was a lot of serious looking into this, and there were ethical practices, there were codes of behaviour and conduct that are not as closely observed today, because in a sense it's a different era. It's not comparable.

I mean a lot of people back in the 1800s and 1900s, their families were sitting in Victorian seance circles. It was a totally different era. Nowadays it's not as known. I mean it's all sensationalized. So people don't learn the ethics that come with it — you know how delicate a circle is.

JOHN: Well, it's pushed to the margins, right, of either being completely denied or just being entertainment. And then it's not taken as seriously.

BROUGH: Well, it's like I've said before, psychics and prostitutes are the same tax code.

JOHN: Yes. It's an underworld. And that's when the frauds are able to slip in there.

BROUGH: It's so unmonitored and unregulated. So, Laron's like, "You have to represent integrity, because this is something that has been lost in this field." Which is interesting. I haven't ever really thought of it that way, but I think that makes sense to me.

She wants to clarify that the entity that we've been working with — she's going to leave it up to the entity to explain its identity. But it's less in touch with our time. So she's been working with it to not wake you up — so that our time is a little more respected.

JOHN: Oh, interesting. So the waking up early—

BROUGH: It's not intentional.

JOHN: So that was to do with our work.

BROUGH: Yup. Absolutely to do with our work, but what Laron's been saying — and your guide with Laron, like, both the girls — are working with it, to help it understand—

JOHN: Understand daily schedules and things.

BROUGH: Yeah. They can be the liaison, as it were.

JOHN: Wow. I asked one night, "Can I just sleep till six, or seven even?" And some mornings I don't mind getting up really early. It's just, if it happens a lot, then obviously it inhibits my ability to function.

BROUGH: Yeah, exactly.

Do you have any questions while we have Laron present?

JOHN: I tried the meditation. So first couple times, it was before bed, and so I just immediately passed out as soon as I relaxed.

BROUGH: That's normal, she says.

JOHN: Yeah. And then, so I've found now the morning seems like a good time. I tried it just this morning, wasn't able to focus quite as much, but—

BROUGH: She's pointing out that Brough does the same thing. I do it in the mornings. So you tried it this morning but you felt you didn't succeed?

JOHN: But I tried it yesterday morning, which was really interesting. I dedicated almost an hour to it, and I felt some effects from it. I think it's the concept of actively relaxing the different parts of my body, which takes a bit of work, getting used to.

'Cause I already feel my body — I feel I'm able to relax my body fairly quickly, and I'm trying to figure out, *Am I relaxed?* I'm not sure, I don't know.

But I feel it went well; I went to the white-light part and I could feel a power coming in, and I almost felt a lifting effect. I could feel sort of surges of power coming in. And I've had that feeling before, even without meditating, these spasms coming into my body, just if I'm lying there, just like electric jolts coming in.

BROUGH: What some have referred to as the Kundalini experience.

JOHN: Oh, oh yeah. Yes, these jolts of electricity. And then, yeah some kind of power coming in.

BROUGH: She's explaining that spirit guides and family oftentimes feed us spiritual energy. Positive energy, healing energy, calming energy. Subtle energies that are not classified by any physical laws that we have, or they're not energies that we know about; they're subtle energies.

JOHN: Yeah. Yeah, I've definitely felt that many times. And then, yeah, this violet sort of shape up above my forehead. Which partly I felt was just a regular optical effect, a biological effect or something, but it seemed like it was a little more pronounced than that.

BROUGH: She's showing me that it's an awakening of your clairvoyant abilities. She's claiming that this meditation was designed to be exactly that, in preparation for future meditations, which will teach astral projection.

JOHN: Yes. Wow.

BROUGH: So you're being prepared, and your guide is working with you.

JOHN: Yeah and I tried to sort of speak with her. As they were saying, as the exercise was specifying. And when I spoke to her, that's when the purple/violet started to appear.

BROUGH: There you go. Yeah. It's good that we're having this dialogue just for the sake of the book. It's like, this progresses the story. And the reader will be practising with you, so your experiences will relate to some of the reader's experiences, or give them a guide. And it's very, very good, so it's really great that you're practising it for the purpose of the book.

JOHN: Yeah so people can follow along.

BROUGH: But she says your guide is working with you. I see her — when you're laying down and you're meditating — I see almost a string of shimmering energy going into your forehead.

And whatever part of the frontal lobe is connected to clairvoyance and all the other psychic faculties, ESP — it's being fed energy and it's being developed. Like neurons and neural pathways and things are being opened. So it's part of a psychic development.

JOHN: Amazing.

BROUGH: And it's just your willingness, your little willingness to do that, that allows your guide to guide, to really work with you. 'Cause they would never force that kind of development on somebody.

JOHN: Right. Yeah, I was never a *meditation* guy, I mean I tried it in my teenage years and enjoyed it and noticed some effects from it in terms of my everyday frame of mind. But I like the fact that it's active, it's not just removing everything. I mean, you're clearing yourself, but it's to extend beyond.

BROUGH: Laron just said that it's to go within.

JOHN: Yeah, yeah.

BROUGH: And in a sense, have a reprieve from the material world. Like taking a break.

JOHN: Yeah and I like that it's sort of something I look forward to. This little reprieve.

BROUGH: Yeah, yeah, it's a perfect word for it, the *reprieve*. But also, like you said, it's an activity to develop, it's a means to an end. Transcendental meditation, that was just always about being quiet and clear and still in your mind. I found that dumb too, but to be fair, and what I realize now, is that all different kinds of meditation have different benefits. Like we said, that may not be for us right now, but this kind of meditation is important for what we're doing.

JOHN: Yeah, and I suppose I can't see meditation ever being a harmful thing for anyone. I think I just wasn't interested before. I think I've always thought of myself as meditative anyway. I always make sure I leave work and go for walks by the lake, or I'll just sit there on the couch and relax, sometimes.

BROUGH: Well, Laron's pointing out you may have meditated in past lives and not known it, because you are naturally adept.

JOHN: Right. I see. Past lives, interesting. That's a topic to get into. I noticed that came up in the last session.

BROUGH: Oh, she's clarifying something for me. Hold on, I got news. She said that there's been some talk amongst them about this book, just to help lighten the load and to give things in a more structured manner, to consider if we want to make this book about relationships and do our original idea of a series of different subjects.

Because it seems that the entity wants me to tap into more detail about some of the concepts. Because there's too many things unfinished. Too many ideas that are posed but don't go anywhere. And it wants to wrap all of it up.

JOHN: I agree with that.

BROUGH: Yeah, okay. 'Cause it wants to focus on *relationship* solely. And the technology and all the other stuff we mentioned are teasers.

JOHN: Yeah. I completely agree with that. I like the idea of going in-depth on something.

BROUGH: Yeah, that's what she's suggested. So, they've been talking about that, and that's one of the reasons why there's been sort of a standby on our channellings.

JOHN: Okay. So they're working out the format.

BROUGH: They are, and they're finding different ways for me to access that information. Just remember, I'm limited to what I'm ready for. So they're finding ways to pose it to us that I can access it. And they wanted to have this talk today, where we agree with them. They don't want to do anything without us agreeing.

JOHN: I agree. What do you think, Brough Perkins?

BROUGH: Uh, I second that motion. The house's vote is unanimous.

JOHN: Motion tabled.

BROUGH: Speaker, you have had your two minutes. Speaker.

Laron's saying there's diamonds in the rough. As you restructure the material for editing, you're going to be polishing the jewels. And she said that it's a developmental process — as future books come out, we're going to keep developing and accessing deeper information. So it's a process. And it has the potential to be a two-fold thing. She says it can teach people about the realities of channelling, that's number one, and it can also teach people the content of the material.

So it's a two-fold thing. And it's supposed to be looked at like a spiritual gift. It's like a present coming from above. It's given in the spirit of being helpful, inspirational, calming, interesting, and just some brain food. Some soul food as it were. So, she wants to just say that that's her interpretation of what the dialogue is.

The book could even be called *The Dialogues*. Because of the form of the channelling. It's Laron's idea — she hasn't covered it with the team. [*Laughs.*] But *The Dialogues*, dot, dot, dot — 'cause this isn't like automatic writing; this is done through spoken word, and it is very much a two-way conversation.

JOHN: Yeah, that is a big difference.

BROUGH: Laron says she's stepping back because she's going to get prepared for my clients. Because she's got their relatives with her.

[*We stop recording and get into the topic of what Laron does behind the scenes to prepare for Brough's readings. I then start a new recording and ask Brough to recap what he was saying.*]

BROUGH: I used to have a belief system that when I did a psychic reading on a client, when I saw things about their life, their past, their future, their relationship, all that life stuff, I thought it was just me scanning and shining beams into their soul and being able to read and interpret them myself. And then when their dead loved ones would come through and talk to me, that's when Laron, my spirit guide, actually played more of an active role in the reading.

But I've since learned, since we started doing these channellings, more about how guides work 'cause Laron's been revealing it. And actually, before every reading, everything I see about a person, it's all pre-set by the guides; they actually come up with a script. So my guide, Laron, meets with the client's spirit guide. Kind of like in Hollywood — your people talk to my people, like our agents are talking about a deal. And so the client's guide gives my spirit guide a script of that person's life.

JOHN: Oh, so she's actually talking to their guide. So there's this whole network happening.

BROUGH: It's a network, yes.

JOHN: Amazing.

BROUGH: And she even said, "You'd be surprised that clients find you based on spirit guidance." Clients are brought to me, like there's a part that they have to play.

JOHN: Like the client might see your television show or hear about it through word of mouth, and that's all guided.

BROUGH: Right. Well, one of the reports in this city — and I'm not boasting, it's true, my clients tell me all the time — they'll say to their hairdresser, "Oh, I'm going to go see a psychic this week," and the hairdresser goes, "Oh, is it Brough?" And they have no way of knowing. Like this happens constantly.

JOHN: You get told this?

BROUGH: I hear it almost every month, that a client had a funny synchronicity where someone that they knew, they didn't know that that person knew of me, but they all know me. I'm really well known in this field.

But now, when dead loved ones — your grandma or your father or whoever's died — come through, it's your dead loved ones talking to my spirit guide, Laron. And Laron helps them come up with a script 'cause the way they communicate to me, the way they reach me, is through pictures and imagery. That's why on the W5 show I said it's like playing charades with the dead.

So Laron was pointing out, let's say, someone's father wants to talk to his daughter on Earth, who's coming to see me. So he died a year ago, and he says, "I want to make contact with my daughter." Laron goes, "What you need to do, Fred, is you have to show Brough a picture, and I'm going to help you. So let's start." So she runs them through a list, like, "What's the date of your death? February nineteenth? Okay, so I'm going to show Brough the number 19, and then I'm going to show him the number 2, and I'm going to give him a feeling of winter because he knows that 2 usually means the second month of the year, and then I'm gonna make him say 'nineteen.' And then hopefully, your daughter will realize that we're talking about the day of your death."

And then Fred's like, "Oh, wow, this is hard, this is more complicated than I thought." And Laron's like, "It's just the way it works." So she counsels them beforehand. And they come up with a whole script of what they want to say to convey the essence or idea of survival of continued consciousness.

So in some ways it's limited. You can almost think of the old telegraphs. It's telegraphs from the dead. That's really what this kind of mediumship is, mental mediumship. So I've learned that that's how it works — since we've been doing the channelling I've been getting more insight about that. It's a very involved process, and I have a lot more respect for my spirit guide than I used to.

Earlier you were saying, a normal person who doesn't do psychic readings, their spirit guide is probably a lot less busy. And Laron actually told me, it's akin to — 'cause I love *Star Trek* — she said basically I'm serving on the starship *Enterprise*, which is the flagship, whereas there are other starships in *Star Trek* where it's just a ship that does runs for cargo and transport. So she was giving me a little wink and a nod to my *Star Trek* love, she's like, "I'm on the *Enterprise*!" 'Cause I'm the starship *Enterprise* for her. She's doing a big gig. She's on the flagship.

JOHN: A central hub.

BROUGH: Yeah. You would be a part of that too. You're the "Number One." The handsome bearded Riker, who gets all the women.

JOHN: And you're bald Picard?

BROUGH: Yeah, bald. Anyway. Not to digress.

JOHN: So they work out a script of symbols.

BROUGH: Yeah, symbols. And if they don't get in touch with Laron — I've even had this happen in readings, where some spirits don't want to cooperate, they just want to talk normally. And I can't do my job, I can't get them clearly, not as clearly as ones who properly communicate. And one of the things I've noticed, at least from the generations I deal with, people in their forties and fifties — so their parents whom they are contacting would have been born in the 1930s and '40s — I find that women communicate better in spirit than men of that era.

But young men who died recently, like when I get fifteen-year-olds or twenty-one-year-olds from today's era, they seem to come through clearly as well. And it's because men of a certain era didn't have an emotional way of conveying information.

JOHN: So their psychological habits carry through.

BROUGH: They carry through. And this form of communication, let's just say, is not ideal for logical-minded people. Even though I'm a logical-minded person.

JOHN: Yes. We're talking right-brained versus left-brained. It's more of a creative form, an associative form.

BROUGH: Correct. Whereas women are able to — through societal measure and through the way they psychologically evolved — convey thought with emotion easily. Men almost segregate or separate emotion, filtering it out of their thought. Men from a certain era. I don't do that, and I don't believe you do that.

JOHN: Well, when you look at the history of mediumship, great mediums, a lot of them are women. I don't know if there have been more women than men or not. The Oracle at Delphi was a woman.

BROUGH: And gay men. Yeah, you're right. But, like, you know, when we get going on our laugh tracks and we're funny with each other, that's a frequency that works really well for mediumship.

JOHN: That's the feeling I always had too, that we're opening it up.

BROUGH: Loosening things up. Loosening the collar.

JOHN: As opposed to being stern.

BROUGH: Yeah. There's nothing sombre. We're not sitting in some dark Victorian seance room, all serious.

JOHN: Like the old black-and-white photos, where even the children have no joy.

* * *

Our next attempt was on the afternoon of Sunday, March 27, 2016. Our entity started straight into a lesson on the topic of thought. Following some discussion, there would come what we would thereafter refer to as "the big reveal."

BROUGH: Okay, I'm sensing something. Channel open.

VOICE: We are, of course, always with you. As far away as a wish or a thought.

Thought is the topic of the day.

It is a human predilection to categorize and box things in, as it were. To create labels that separate and ultimately subjugate. It's surprising to me that you don't label your labels, with all the labelling that you do.

An idea to be posed today is that cohesive thinking, with a steady, beautiful, flowing stream of peaceful thought, is an ideal to strive for, especially in your world in human form. Most people, individuals, carry on about their lives with the assumption that only their actions and words are what they're accountable for, but their thoughts are random nothings that bounce around between their skull. This is a concept I have mentioned before. And that indeed they don't have any responsibility or control over their thinking.

In fact, the opposite is true — that if you control only your thinking, your actions and words become more fluid and consistent and begin to flow from you beautifully and eloquently. If you spend most of your time, if not all of your time, operating on the assumption that if you learn to control your thinking, the rest of your life would fall into place effortlessly, it would be a good thing indeed.

This level of responsibility — personal responsibility — frightens most people. Most people choose, often unconsciously, to remain in their soul coma, or soul sleep, throughout lifetimes, never awakening to the realization that thought is a power in and of itself to be utilized; a tool, as it were, that is at your disposal. Perhaps your most precious tool.

After all, it was said once that "I think, therefore I am." If you pay attention to your thinking, you will notice, eventually, that you use thought to separate yourself from others. You think yourselves apart.

Whether it is "She is over there and I am over here" or "He thinks about things this way and I think about things that way," all of these separation ideas are nothing more than ideas, constructs of your own doing, often handed to you by your predecessors.

In each individual there must come a time for a thought liberation, as it were, or an emancipation of thought, of free thinking, to rise out of the box that you have constructed for yourselves. You begin to practise looking at every other individual, including plants, animals, bugs, all life, as being interconnected with you on a deep fundamental level. This is a concept people have heard of but few ever understand.

When you work on the level of thought, you have discovered the potential to change your perceptions, finally. When you have changed your perceptions, that eventually goes all the way back to changing your core beliefs.

There are many, many individuals in your world today who believe that thinking positively can have direct and immediate effects on the outcomes of their lives. This philosophy, or belief, is not a bad one inherently, as it always points back to thought being important, thought as being principal. It brings you within your own head, as it were. And in that way, it is a good concept.

However, no amount of positive thoughts or affirmations can directly affect your reality if your beliefs have stayed the same. An example of this would be someone who thinks positively and wishes for a great deal of money to come their way, while they maintain the deeply entrenched belief that they are inherently unworthy. Whether it is unworthy of love, appreciation, acknowledgement, wealth — these deep-seated beliefs are what truly govern what you can magnetically pull toward yourself.

Just as with anything in life, in order to become proficient at something, you must practise. Practise to become an explorer of thought, an observer of the depth of your own mind. Some have said, an examined person.

Eventually you will become proficient enough to reach the core of your belief systems, much like a central nexus. And from there, with a gentle hand and knowledge of spiritual law and principles, you will be able to restructure your belief systems. At which point, within days, hours, even minutes, you will see effects start to ripple throughout your life.

For it is your fundamental belief systems that act much like a computer program, or a computer virus, which can affect directly the outcomes and the flow of experiences into and throughout your life and the lives of those close to you.

There have been many books and many philosophies written in your world about examining thought and changing your thought forms. It is not necessary for us to attempt to reinvent the wheel here today. However, I merely am pointing, as a signpost would, to an area of exploration that would benefit any and all explorers of reality to venture toward. Indeed, as you begin to form artificial intelligence in your world, it will trigger a sort of new thought wave, a new revival of interest in thinking and psychology.

As is the case most often with human beings, you need to have your insides splayed out in front of you before you'll finally take notice of them. There are much quicker and simpler ways, but you are resistant. It's not entirely your fault. The mind is only ready for what the mind is ready for. We've said before, you do not feed steak to babies, that would be detrimental; they require pablum.

Those of you who are ready and capable of hearing this message will begin to explore and deal with your level of thought. And as you face your thoughts, challenge them and change them through using spiritual principles, you will get deeper and deeper into the thoughts that were once unconscious, but as they begin to be revealed to you through your dreams and your daily lives, you will be able to address them and change them, alter your beliefs, eventually, and begin to see true, worthwhile effects start to play out.

Earlier it was mentioned that positive thinking is a belief system, which is true. The beauty of undoing your negative thoughts and your negative beliefs is that positive thinking becomes a side effect: You no longer have to try to be positive or try to smile or try to be kind or try to be loving. You just are, you simply are, when you get the negative out of the way.

So in a sense it is a waste of time to try to be positive, and it can be uncomfortable to face your negative side, your dark side, as it were. But if you do, and you successfully heal it, you will find the most miraculous and beautiful surprise, that all that is left is positivity. For that is what you are.

A shadow is not a thing. It is simply a break in the continuity of light. You cannot flick a switch and turn on the dark, as it were. A shadow only exists when something has been placed in the way of light.

Once you take down that blockage, that object is removed, and light streams in and the shadows vanish. It can be said about your darker side, your negative thoughts and your negative beliefs, that they are simply shadows cast through the subconscious mind by the blocks of false beliefs that have been placed in the way of the light that is your soul.

False beliefs, such as

"You are only a body."

"You are not good enough until…"

"You will have happiness when…"

"You are limited because…"

All the things that you've been taught growing up in the physical world that are false have lent themselves to these vast mental constructs, these false belief systems that stop the steady flow of love and joy and spirit. They must all be taken down individually and dealt with on a case-by-case basis within yourself. And only you have the power to do this. No one else can do it for you. Not even God.

Brough has often referred to this as "homework." Something, ironically, he rarely did in school. Your inner work is just as important as the work you do physically in this world to get by each day.

And much like some advanced civilizations that eventually crumbled, their materialism and material work advanced quite far, but their spiritual inner work did not keep up. And a vast imbalance occurred, often leading them to be disconnected from their intuition and their insight, which led to fatal mistakes and the eventual demise of their society and civilization.

The intention here is to highlight the importance of inner homework. Of course, there are teachers both on our side and in your world. When you are ready, if you put the call out, they will appear and come to your aid, to assist you in this mental homework. You do not even have to say anything out loud or join any message boards on the internet. Simply make a decision in your heart that you wish to become proficient at doing your inner work. And that signal will be received and responded to, every single time. After all, are we not here?

It is nice to speak with you again, John.

JOHN: You too. We missed you.

VOICE: Oh — very sweet. Of course, it is difficult for us to miss you, as we know you will exist forever.

I am aware that the subject of thought was not exactly what you had anticipated today, but I do hope it is a well-received subject.

Before we get to questions, I'd like to expand on my talk about thought.

When you go within on a mental level and address your thought patterns and work to undo your false beliefs, you will, for the first time in your life, begin to have a relationship with yourself.

Many childlike souls in your world who were blessed with the gift of being born into a free country or a free land, who were blessed with relatively good looks and a decent family life, have life almost handed to them on a silver platter — it is almost too easy for them, almost too good. Normal, superficial, surface-level life is appealing to them.

Many of these souls are good souls. Many of them have had difficult previous lives. In a sense, this lifetime is simply a vacation for them. And some of them even find themselves called to spiritual paths of varying degrees. Still, they remain stuck on a superficial level.

We recently inspired Brough to write an article, which he read to you aloud today, about many modern movements of becoming your "authentic self," which of course ties into thought and changing your belief systems.

We had intended, but failed, to imprint upon Brough during that article, that the individuals who subscribe to this movement of becoming an authentic person, which in and of itself seems to be an oxymoron, that they measure authenticity through superficial indicators such as confidence at board meetings, being able to "monetize a passion" — which is a very Western idea, mind you — being able to live along a sunny beach coastal region, driving a certain kind of vehicle or having a certain type of diet regimen.

These superficial ideas are what certain shallow, materialistic individuals feel or believe constitute spiritual living. None of them are inherently bad or good; it's no judgement of them, of course. However, these individuals manage to create a lifestyle where their diet is very good, and perhaps they found a way to start to monetize a passion, ironically often being that they become a life coach.

Rightly so. Of course, they do it well. All the while, teaching their philosophy on authenticity, good diet, monetizing passion, speaking with confidence. Scarcely do they touch on anything of true spiritual value.

And gently, we attempt to guide them. But even through a developed and advanced medium such as Brough, we can have difficulty imprinting our thoughts and our ideas. Because of course, the business of life in a body can be quite distracting. Never forget, we have tremendous compassion for what you go through on a day-to-day basis in your world.

If you ever detect urgency in anything that we transmit to you, please know that the urgency is our will for you to be free and happy. Nothing more, nothing less.

Getting back to the point. As you develop a relationship with yourself through your inner homework, for the first time, you can understand yourself and have compassion for your mistakes. Is it not true and wholly conceivable for you, right now, in this very moment, that the way you look at others will change? That you will no longer make false assumptions as often? That perhaps you will understand why people operate the way they appear to operate, at a deeper level, because you are learning about how *you* operate at a deeper level.

You will end up connecting with others far better, all because you have finally connected with yourself. It is often said in your world that before you can love others, you must love yourself. We covered this in a previous chapter. To drive the point home, loving yourself is not about what you eat or how you monetize. It is not about how pretty your nails or your clothing are. It is about how you *think*. This, unfortunately, is a concept that is not discussed enough by the life coaches.

Ironically for you, John, the Buddhists seem to have this one figured out. Many Buddhist teachers focus solely on thought practice. And they have it quite correct. Unfortunately, the problem with Buddhism is it almost gets too lost in thought and forgets to include the spirit. That is for another discussion.

[I had expressed some reservations about Buddhism in talks with Brough, to do with the point that the entity makes here.]

Due to the constant fragmentation of your mind, the way humans have taught themselves to compartmentalize and separate from everything, what you find happens in your world is that bits and pieces of truth are scattered everywhere, like a broken mirror.

There have been ancient cultures in your world, including most recently the Hopi natives, who have deep-seated core values and beliefs, rooted even in their own language, that wholly and entirely excludes the concept of "separation" altogether. There is no "here" nor "there" nor "you" nor "I" in the Hopi language. It is all spoken in the present; even when they speak about the past, they speak about it in the present.

[I researched the topic briefly and it does appear that there are terms for some of these concepts, including pronouns and denotative words like "he," "she," "it," "they," "those," etc. As far as past and future tenses, while there is a future tense, the past is indeed spoken about using present tense, as stated here. While some Hopi terms may reflect the idea of separation, it is still possible that the core values and beliefs excluded the concept of separation, and some researchers have claimed that the Hopi do not perceive time as flowing linearly from past to present to future. We welcome input from anyone with knowledge of Hopi culture.]

Hopi natives experience a high degree of telepathy, interestingly. And it is no coincidence that they do; their belief systems allow for it. Similar to how Eastern civilizations from India and Asia have a higher rate of children recalling past-life memories. Again, in those cultures, reincarnation is a common belief.

Belief, you see, is not always a bad thing, as long as it is rooted in reality. On the opposite side of the coin, people make-believe all kinds of falsehoods, as with fundamentalists and religious zealots; their beliefs are rooted in and sullied with negative experiences from their childhood and their culture. Their beliefs in a wrathful, vengeful god or deity, for example, that may lead them to do horrific things.

Recently in the United States, a middle-aged gay couple lay sleeping together. A vile religious man poured scalding, burning hot water on them in their bed. They suffered horrific burns. This is just an example of false beliefs at work.

Indeed, if you plant a seed in healthy, fertile soil, with good access to sunlight and water, the byproduct will be a fantastic plant that produces wonderful fruit. If you plant a seed in unhealthy soil, diseased, it will grow and it will barely yield any valuable results. Your beliefs are but a seed that can grow into series of wonderful experiences or experiences of very little value to anyone involved.

It's all about the soil in which you plant them. Do you plant them in fertile, rich soils of spiritual law and reality, or do you plant them in the diseased, fungus-ridden soil of human history and culture?

Now, this is your free will. Oftentimes, when you fail to pay attention to your thoughts, you have forfeited your own free will. What a silly mistake. Much like individuals who fail to vote when they have a chance to lend themselves to changing the direction of their own society, do not forgo or forfeit your own vote when it comes to yourself any longer. Do not wait any longer. Begin today to commit yourself, even if you do not exactly know how.

To begin, pay attention and become vigilant for your thoughts, your thought patterns, ask yourself where they come from, why you believe things that you believe. Question yourself, audit yourself, and implement healthier, happier thought forms when and where you can. For you have the power to change your mind.

Indeed, the truth, at higher levels, is that even thought is no longer necessary. The mind is completely abstract. Thought is simply a byproduct of living in the physical world. You will eventually graduate to a degree where you no longer require thought, and your thoughts are replaced by pure knowledge. This state is a blissful state indeed. Confusion is a thing of the past here.

You wish to discuss something with us today, John?

JOHN: Once you mentioned in one of our sessions that for everything there is a correct and an incorrect use. Can we say then the same for thought, that the problem is not thought itself, the problem is just incorrect thought or unhealthy thought? And so, people shouldn't be feeling that they should not think, just that they should analyze their thoughts and then get to their beliefs through their thoughts.

VOICE: Correct. To further an analogy, think of "thoughts" as apples and the "belief" as being the tree. You start dealing with your apples, or your thoughts, and eventually you will trace yourself back to the tree of belief. And once you are able to change the belief, much like a garden, or cutting away a diseased branch, you can indeed make your whole thought tree a healthy one, producing healthy fruit.

When you change your belief system, you undo false beliefs and replace them with beliefs that are grounded in truth, love, spiritual law — not to be confused with religious law, mind you. Then what you will have as a natural byproduct are positive thoughts. You don't have to try to be loving, you don't have to try to be positive anymore. When your beliefs are healthy, your thoughts will naturally be healthy.

It is a futile game to judge yourself, condemn yourself, and start to feel and propagate further guilt by looking at your thoughts and deeming them unworthy. Your thoughts are simply byproducts, side effects. They're not your fault, in a sense.

But using thought, tracing the route of thought back to the belief tree, and then addressing your beliefs — asking yourself where you found them originally, why they're there, and summarily dismissing the ones that are of no value and replacing them with new, informed belief systems based on truth, love, and happiness, science and philosophy — your thoughts will become beautiful precious jewels that will reign throughout your life like a prince bathing in riches.

Many who experience this type of a transformation call it an awakening, and indeed it is; it is the beginning of an awakening. Some happen upon it due to being influenced by a powerful, profound teacher. Whilst others will make their way themselves.

At this current time for yourself, John, you would not listen to a teacher; you don't trust them. Which is just as well because you can become a teacher yourself by doing the hard work. Indeed, there are some children who learn to tie their shoes because they are taught and others who teach themselves.

But perhaps, as an experiment, and we only suggest this with a mild sense of intrigue, you may practise asking yourself why you have a visceral reaction to teachers. For that is rooted in a belief system that you may discover does not serve you. Nevertheless, in tracing that thought pattern back to a belief tree, the irony being, you'll probably just simply become a teacher yourself. [*With a chuckle.*] So you better start to like them.

The point I wanted to highlight here is that the only way to truly have healthy relationships with others is to first have a healthy relationship with yourself. As Brough's guide, Laron, pointed out last time to you, it was my intention to circle back to concepts given in the beginning of this book and expand on them, giving a practical guide for the reader and for you and Brough.

Remember, you're only able to access this information because, on some level, both of you have been doing this homework yourselves; perhaps unconsciously, but nevertheless it is there, and it is advanced homework.

For I have somewhat of a scope into your futures from the position that I occupy in the universe. I wish to assure both of you boys that neither of you will be alone in this lifetime. Both of you, on your destinies and your horizons, have lovers and extended families you have yet to meet, friendships you have yet to develop. And it is with great pleasure and sincerity that I wish to convey to you that you both will remain in each other's lives, closer than ever before, well into old age.

Indeed, the work we do here today helps to solidify and bind that bond. And the words conveyed and expressed, and the way in which you will order them, will have profound therapeutic effects on all eyes that lie upon them, assisting in a sort of freedom from the shackles and binds and bondage that so many people feel self-imposed with today.

For what you call normal is simply what you're used to. Is it not important to have a break from normal once in a while? Perhaps this is why so many people are inherently fascinated by the paranormal — what *you* call the paranormal. Which is not to be confused with "supernatural." The supernatural is a fairy tale, a mythopoetic realm of dreams and ideologies.

The paranormal is the fringe of normal. [*Slowly and emphatically.*] The twilight land. The edge of the ocean that Christopher Columbus never fell off of. Paranormal is extending and probing beyond the known limits and, of course, finding that, indeed, the range of "normal" needs simply to be expanded.

And you pointed out something very astute and very, very true this morning at breakfast when you said to Brough that even when human beings learn, through science and technology, of the existence of alternate dimensions and, indeed, possibly make contact with those dimensions, that the humans of that era will still insist on maintaining a stagnant, staunch, materialistic perspective, where they'll actually try to project their own laws and values into an entirely other dimension.

Of course, that is true — for a time, which you also pointed out. We often see this in our world, on our level of reality, whenever human individuals have a glimpse of our world and they attempt to take the principles and spiritualize matter, as it were. For instance, the favourite saying, "Money is God in motion." If only you knew what money was. It is anything but God. [*With a laugh.*]

Many in your world already understand that there are great, vast systems that you take for granted, such as your monetary system, your economy, which are founded entirely on lies, pyramid schemes, and greed. Tying back, of course, to the seed of belief.

People in the day who created these systems or lent themselves to creating these systems held false beliefs. You see how far-reaching belief systems can go, even when they're false. And how the consequences can be. Indeed, you are your own jailer. But alternatively, you can also be the one who sets yourself free. It all stems back to doing your inner homework.

I apologize for ranting, rambling.

Brough has taken a break from doing readings for several days. It is amazing to note how, when a medium stops doing readings, even for a few days, even when they are as advanced as Brough, they quickly lose confidence in the process. My words aren't coming through as fluently as I'd want them to, but you'll make the necessary corrections in the postscript.

You wish to lead the conversation now?

JOHN: Hm! I'm not sure what to say.

VOICE: We found it to be ironic that we would be having a session like this on your Easter holiday. Do not worry. That's not some allusion to me being Jesus. I am not.

JOHN: So, why do you feel it's ironic?

VOICE: The concept of the holiday being that of a spiritual one as well as a resurrection-based holiday.

Indeed, anytime that we have a successful contact, or a bridge between our world and yours, is it not like a mini-resurrection? Keeping in mind, these concepts and spiritual documents were written in a different language, with different intentions, in a different day and age.

You have been so fond of pointing out the fallacy of people taking things too literally, which we commend you for, John. Excellent observation. People are indeed far too literal.

JOHN: Yeah, and I think that gets to the point of what you were saying about people applying their own values onto, well, parallel dimensions, for example, as you were saying, and when Brough mentioned that one of the ideas was to create economic trading between the parallel dimensions, which is pretty funny.

VOICE: Mm-hm.

JOHN: And I don't even understand how that could possibly work and what it even means, but...

VOICE: The wheels have already begun turning.

JOHN: Yeah. And it shows that we have it in us to want to explore, and we talked about this, Brough and I, in our live event that we did back in October, the whole thing of trying to contact other dimensions using technology and saying how they're using a budget of billions whereas Brough only charges eighty dollars a session.

VOICE: [*Laughs slightly.*]

JOHN: But this idea of contacting other dimensions, I mean it shows that it's obviously something deep in us that we want to do, but these scientists are pursuing it within their framework I guess, within their system of beliefs; they won't allow for contact through consciousness alone, but they will allow for it using a technological means.

Do you see this as something that will bear fruit? Will this lead to something fruitful?

VOICE: There are entities overseeing such experiments, with the power to intercede and stop certain results from occurring if humanity isn't ready or puts itself in danger, unwittingly of course.

And so, indeed, these experiments are not entirely objective and empirical, although you think they are.

You've been introduced to the concept of some of these entities as being higher beings or what various other people might call "angels." Indeed, I don't want to digress and get too far into that subject today. That is for another book entirely.

But yes, it is similar to your ITC experimentation, which greatly assisted in your advancement in your own mediumistic abilities. The results from ITC, although profound and convincing to a materialistic mind, are far less detailed than the results accomplished through direct mediumship, except in the rare few cases where you have a group of people creating a synergistic effect, or as you would call it, a contact field. They were able to get full phone calls and conversations with the dead.

In most cases, ITC gives you short, blip-like messages, transmissions, often in code words. And in as far as that is valuable to mediumship, to the bereft who have lost loved ones, experiments with your particle accelerators will be valuable, in increments. Again, the experiments themselves are limited and the technology itself is limited only because the inspiration and the ideas behind it stem from rigid belief systems. They can only handle small increments. A more advanced, open mind might be able to come up with an experiment that would bring and yield greater results.

In a sense, it all comes down to going about things in an organic way or a technological way; and when put together, the two can be quite complementary to one another, which I believe is where you're getting at with your line of inquiry. But due to the rigid, close-minded, inflexible belief systems of said scientists, of course as you had made the point without meaning to, or perhaps without saying it, they would not take seriously the organic approach.

It is too bad, because many of the scientists who have had textbooks written about them, in the early days, even before the Industrial

Revolution, were in many ways more inspired, less rigid, more flexible, and able to have better ideas. Take for example your Nikola Tesla. Oh, how he would have some bright ideas.

JOHN: Even Tesla was sometimes constrained by the worry of being seen to believe in psychic phenomena. Because I think he did have some cases where he predicted things, like he predicted a train accident where he told people not to get on a train, and things like that, but he would also distance himself from that type of thinking and say he was a materialist. So, I think he himself had maybe a bit of a conflict in his mind there. Because he was kind of on the border between being a mystic and a technical person, an engineer.

VOICE: Oh, only in the public persona. He wasn't really on the border in his personal self. His main fascination was non-locality, something that you take for granted in your wireless world today. The concept of psychic phenomena was not at all a far stretch for someone who believed in non-locality, in non-local phenomena, which for the reader, means to be able to send messages through thin air without any mechanical means, without any wires or cables or copper string.

JOHN: Radio.

VOICE: Exactly, yes, radio is a non-local event.

JOHN: And he wanted to send power without wires, that was one of his dreams. To send electricity through the air.

VOICE: Correct.

JOHN: But as you said, as humans, we sometimes need to have our innards splayed out in front of us!

VOICE: Correct.

JOHN: And so, is this "contacting parallel dimensions" idea through physical means — and I'm not talking about ITC, that's a little different, but I'm talking about the CERN particle accelerator and that type of thing — because they can't get there through their belief systems? The idea of contacting non-physical worlds, are they then splaying out their innards in this way through technology? Still trying to get to that same goal, but because they can't do it through their belief systems in an organic way, they have to do it this way. Do you see that as what's happening?

VOICE: Partially, yes. But you have within your grasp technological means to create devices which would, no pun intended, blow your mind. To return to Tesla for a moment, try to imagine in his day the idea of anything being wireless, of being able to transmit voice or music or sound through the air without any tools or implementations that are physical. It is truly a foreign concept; very, very, very few human beings could even wrap their minds around such an idea in those days.

Tesla's belief systems were open enough, porous enough for him to step outside the conventions of the time and predict and imagine something that is quite commonplace in your world today. He was in many ways ahead of his time.

And that was simply due to the fact that he did not maintain rigid, strict belief systems that were limiting and self-imposed. Indeed, throughout his life he worked to change his belief systems. He was a fan of philosophy, as well as science, as well as art. He was a man of many talents; what you might call a Renaissance man.

Perhaps naive in his personal dealings with people — because of that lack of rigidity, the openness of heart — he was often taken advantage of and blatantly abused, revealing secrets to the wrong individuals, opening himself up to retaliation from jealous minds, who themselves were too limited by their own rigidity.

It is no surprise that now in the astral, Tesla himself is taking a well-deserved vacation and revelling in the bliss of having no physical responsibilities whatsoever. It is wonderful to be free from a body.

Anyway, back to the topic at hand. Do you wish to expand on your question?

JOHN: No, I don't think so. Do you feel that we covered things enough? Regarding your original topic of thought, do you feel that we covered it sufficiently or do you want to go through anything further on that?

VOICE: Oh yes, I feel it is covered.

Perhaps in the next session, we'll open it with another mind practice. Not unlike a meditation, but perhaps a step further. Something that will allow you to implement changes to your thought patterns.

JOHN: Okay, yeah.

As we discussed with Laron last week, I tried the meditation a few times. I like doing it; I look forward to doing it. And I've learned to do it in the mornings.

[*I describe the meditation, how the violet form is getting more complex, pulsating.*]

VOICE: Yes. Your clairvoyance is expanding, developing. You're seeing subtle energies. Oh, how mystical and marvellous you appear. Just think for a moment of all the wavelengths of light and energy that you cannot see with your physical eyes. There is even more than you know. More subtle energies.

When you're feeling love toward a child or an animal or another person, how your heart and chest radiate the warm glow. Or when you tend to an ill person, your hands seem to vibrate and radiate. Beautiful, beautiful, sparkling, shimmering colours. What mystical, fascinating creatures you are. What soulful beings you are, and you don't even know it, because you trust too much in your physical eyes and not enough in your spirit.

Each and every person, especially the ones who don't know it, are heroes, to be regarded with admiration. Each on a journey, a quest, to assist in a larger tapestry of events playing out.

JOHN: What are those events? I mean, is that something we will get into?

VOICE: Absolutely. Perhaps at a later time.

Of course, at the level I exist, I have no personal need or attachment to giving myself an identity. However, in the interest of good reading and to tell a story, as it were, I feel perhaps it would be beneficial to introduce myself formally to you.

My image, my likeness, the concept of who I am, is celebrated and regarded most heavily in your eastern culture of India, as a spiritual entity known as Shiveya.

Considered to be the god of death, I never thought of myself as a god or even a guru. Of course, they have made me out to be a man when I was a woman in my incarnation. That happened a lot more than you realize, by the way. Many famous figures who you regard as men were actually women.

I am a soul who could be considered a teacher at this state. Within the group, you exist, as well as Brough and many others who are pupils. For whatever reason — why ever do the Earth and Mars and Jupiter orbit your sun? — our souls seem to orbit each other. I was the principal being in charge of orchestrating, choreographing, synchronicities between you all. And I remain vigilant and protective of all of you as if you were my very own.

Do you recall when Brough told you once that he believed he had a dream when he was around the age of eight, walking the streets of India, and there were beggars and homeless people at his feet? And he was trying to give them everything he had. But as he ran out of food himself and money, they just kept pulling at him more and more and more until he was brought to his knees, into the filth, surrounded by suffering.

He awoke from that dream profoundly affected by it, at only the age of eight, not really understanding or having any prior knowledge of the state of India, much less why he himself would have any kind of a subconscious connection there. But he did indeed have a past life there. It wasn't his most previous one. It is why, also, he is fond of Mother Teresa, who was drawn there, within my sole principality as well.

For our group, in many ways, is part of a bigger plan to help be the catalyst of change. As part of the lore or mythology surrounding my identity, my disciples carry weapons they would never use. Warriors of peace.

Approximately ten years later, when Brough was eighteen years old, during a morning meditation very similar to the ones that you do, he noticed an apparition as clear as day, of an Indian boy, no older than the age of eleven, wearing a golden robe, staring up at some unseen light source as the light was shining down on him. In this instance, Brough felt very much that this child was somehow paying respect to him, at the same time, looking up above both of them to the higher entity. Of course, this is one of my children of the light, who exists currently in this time frame or this level of reality and is part of the same soul group. This was a few years before you and Brough began to see the 22s.

Then a year later, Brough had a detailed dream while he was practising out-of-body experiences, where he felt two cats run across his chest before he lifted out of his body — the souls of which are his current cats, that I was planning to send to him. His familiars, if you will. And in that dream, he fell to my feet and met two beings, which were very high beings, very, very advanced beings, perhaps at the end of their cycles of incarnation.

One was a tall blond long-haired individual by the name of Rayne, and the other a fair-complexioned girl who was Rayne's soul mate. Brough at the time was suffering his first heartbreak from a relationship that ended. It had past-life connotation to it. It was a repeat lesson of the previous time. So it had affected him to the core.

He shared with me his experience, and I explained not to worry, that I would remain with him, but that times ahead would be much, much, much more difficult. It was in that experience that I informed him of my identity as Shiveya. Of course, he was so cute and young, he ended up calling me She-Ra, after a popular television character in your world. Although, I can't say the comparison was too off the mark. How interestingly the subconscious works.

Oh, my young Brough. I'm thankful to say he has come through the worst of my predictions. He is now on the home stretch to healing. Only a couple years after that, and you can verify this information with Brough's father himself, Brough's parents — his mother was still alive at this time — witnessed a full-body apparition, a tall blond-haired young man, appear in their room. At first Brough's father thought it was Brough. Of course, when the apparition walked through the wall, it became apparent to Brough's father that what he was dealing with was literally out of this world.

John Perkins [*Brough's father*] began to see this apparition several times, but it was too frightening for him to face. The consequences of such a thing existing would shatter John Perkins's entire perception of the world and reality. At the time that was too much of a notion for him to handle. And like any agent of love or representative of spirit, if not wanted or if it is not welcome or [*the receiver of the experience is not*] ready, it will leave. So, when this being stepped through the wall, it appeared in an alternate universe, a parallel dimension, perhaps one where John was more ready for its visage. Where it could make contact with and perhaps alter the timeline to save Brough's mother's life. Indeed, I did send one of my souls, one of my warriors, to help alter the timeline.

And remember we are all equals under God. We all have free will. You can present someone with knowledge or medicine, and if they refuse to embrace it, there's very little that can be done. According to the laws of love you must be patient.

The tall blond soul is indeed the higher self of Brough, the future version. Perhaps a final lifetime, if you will. One where he has completed most, if not all, of his lessons and is ready to return home and become a great teacher of love. Like any being of love, before it makes its final step, it reaches back through all the lifetimes and all the experiences and struggles, in one last-ditch attempt to spread as much healing, help alleviate as much pain as it possibly can. Indeed, many of you on Earth who felt that your lives were saved by some unseen force or an angel, indeed, have experienced your future selves reaching backward through time to help yourselves. To open the way for further advancement.

For in the end it all comes down to you. And I remain at the gateway. The edge of the farthest reach of the last star. To help guide and be present for you as you make your journeys one by one into awakening, to a return to love. For just as I have ascended and outgrown the need for physical existence, you as well will reach the same destination. For all of us are one, all of us brothers and sisters equal in value and in power. It is only your limiting beliefs that hold you back from being able to remember your true selves.

And so, with that, I send you love. I'm aware that Brough will need some time to digest this information. But please know that physical identity, human labels, mean as much to me as a retirement fund. I have zero use for them; I have no attachment to them. My only concern is your welfare and your state of mind.

Many blessings, and we will speak again.

JOHN: Thank you.

BROUGH: Girls! You were sent to daddy. [*Speaking to the cats.*]

Okay so that was my version of your "Blinded by the Light" session.

JOHN: Revelation of things in your past.

BROUGH: Did I ever tell you about my dad seeing the apparition?

JOHN: Yeah, you did. But not some of those details.

BROUGH: We got a demigod on our hands. This is a class-24 full roam-ranging apparition. Cross-dimensional rift. Get our proton packs ready.

JOHN: I don't think we've got this one in the database.

BROUGH: This is not in *Tobin's spirit Guide*.

JOHN: So, I recently became friends with someone called Shveta.

BROUGH: Really.

JOHN: And I had a synchronicity about her name. I was watching some show and it was talking about someone with that same name, Shveta, with a "t" — and it said she's the key or something like that. And I thought it was talking about her, the person I had met. That was a week or two ago.

BROUGH: And that was recent?

JOHN: That synchronicity was maybe a couple weeks ago.

BROUGH: And I've never heard you deal with anyone with a name similar.

JOHN: Never. She was a recruiter that I was talking to about jobs and we had lunch.

BROUGH: You should make notes about that in this chapter. Because your synchronicities help tie this all together. Shveta, and this idea that Shiveya would be a female.

JOHN: Oh — because you've been getting a male presence this whole time. So, was that just an impression?

BROUGH: It doesn't matter, because it isn't male or female really, at that level. But it said in its last incarnation it was female.

JOHN: Female, and then was later portrayed as male.

BROUGH: Which has happened a lot.

JOHN: And it said you were already aware of this being.

BROUGH: I had that experience, yeah.

JOHN: And you had a name for them.

BROUGH: I called it "She-Ra" after the He-Man character.

JOHN: So, this isn't something brand new then—

BROUGH: This is old. I just never connected the dots. It all sort of plays out as a big tapestry now. I dunno. I'll have to listen to all this again. It's getting interesting…

JOHN: Well, it's funny 'cause I was going to bring that up, because Laron had mentioned this potential revelation, and then just as soon as I thought it — I keep thinking "he" but now I'm thinking "she." I like the idea of "she" — because we don't have any women in our group. I like the idea that there's a female presence.

BROUGH: But I don't detect gender. I don't detect identity with it; it doesn't even seem human, that's why I call it the entity. But I guess now I could just call it Shiveya. Shivs. Shiver me timbers.

I don't know how I feel about this. I'm ready to maybe wrap up and not do this anymore.

JOHN: No, you're not.

BROUGH: I'm not thrilled about the concept of channelling a demigod. It's just not exactly what I had planned for my career.

JOHN: But that's just a category.

BROUGH: That's the belief-system thing. You're right.

JOHN: I mean it's still the same person or entity that we were channelling before.

I wanted to understand more of the history of who this is. You're saying "demigod," but why are you saying that?

BROUGH: Oh, because it's at this high level of astral plane or spiritual plane. We've heard dead people and channellings and seances say that there are higher realms. We've heard this. So, this sort of place. And I keep seeing visions when I'm doing this with you. And I don't see any imagery, like, I don't have access; it's just blank, it's just empty space. And it's not really like that, it's just I can't get it.

JOHN: There's no form, or not in a way we can perceive it.

BROUGH: And my mind isn't ready to perceive what is there, or something. So, this energy, yeah. And it having some perspective on our futures. It said something about us not being alone, right?

JOHN: Oh — yes, that's right. Partners and so on.

BROUGH: So, we're going to get predictions throughout this. Wow, okay. What are your thoughts and feelings on this latest contact?

JOHN: I don't know — I don't really have any — I'm a bit blank today. There's a different feeling today. I didn't feel it was going to be a big dialogue session and I didn't want to ask a bunch of questions. And I had a sense that it wasn't interacting with us in the same way, it was a bit more distant. And it said its words weren't coming through as well. But at the same time there was an intensity going on. Maybe that's why I was acting a little weird before. I was getting quite giddy. But I knew it wasn't going to be a big dialogue session.

BROUGH: Yeah, because it had intended to go and revisit some ideas from earlier.

JOHN: Yes, that's right. But also, this revelation. I feel that was just the tip of the iceberg of our understanding who it is. But it's funny, she was saying — I'm going to say "she"; I can't say "it" — she was saying about labels, and talking about how people put labels on their labels.

BROUGH: Oh, isn't that interesting — it was going on about labels and stuff, and it knew that it was going to reveal who it was.

JOHN: It seems like it was leading up to that. And telling us it really isn't all that important, but really basically for good reading, she said.

BROUGH: For interest's sake.

JOHN: Well, I guess it helps, right? Cause otherwise we just keep saying "the entity" or whatever — it helps identify a source. "Names mean about as much to me as a retirement fund." That's amazing.

BROUGH: It's a pun on being dead, I guess?

JOHN: It's just funny as hell. I just love it.

I'm processing it. They said you're going to need time to digest, and I do too. But a lot of that was about stuff that's happened with you. So, I'll write it up, but you can also listen back. But it might be easier for you to sit down with it and read it.

BROUGH: Yeah, it will be. I'm a little emotional about my girls being sent to me because it dawned on me that I got these girls around the time of my mother's death. And I knew that the entity I encountered predicted that things would be more difficult.

JOHN: Explain that again. Go over what happened.

BROUGH: Well, I was attempting out-of-body experiences around age nineteen. I had been heartbroken about my ex, and he cut me off, so I was attempting to leave my body so I could spy on him essentially. You know how normal humans do a drive-by outside their ex's house? I would do an astral fly-by.

JOHN: Psychic stalking.

BROUGH: But the phenomenon that always successfully occurred when I was out of my body was, I couldn't think of my ex, I was so damn happy. And that was what tuned me in to realizing how powerful hormones and body stuff is. 'Cause when I was in astral, I had to force myself to remember that I even cared about going to my ex's!

And anyway, I made it out and I guess these girls [*the cats*] were running across my chest, which is exactly what they do now by the way. This morning they were chasing each other, running over me in bed. And I sort of interpreted that to be a spirit taking the form of a cat. But it wasn't, I guess, however it works.

And I met this small Pygmy-looking woman. She looked dark, like an Indian, and she had a bowl haircut, and she was very small. And she was sitting on kind of a throne, but a wide throne, like a love-seat throne.

JOHN: So this was after you left your body. Did you go to a particular place? Did you go off somewhere?

BROUGH: I went to a hall or a monastery, and she was on some kind of throne, and she had this booming voice. And I said, "Who are you?" And she goes, "Shiveya"! And I go, "She-Ra?" And she goes, "No, Shiveya."

JOHN: Wow — this is incredible that this links up to something you had happen.

BROUGH: I've met it. It took the form of this Pygmy person. The rainforest Pygmy people. Have you ever seen the Pygmy people?

JOHN: Yeah.

BROUGH: And the tall guy and the girl were there and I was really attracted to them both. And they took me on this long walk across what looked like Irish hillsides. And they were just talking to me for hours, telling me about life and the universe, and they were referring to Shiveya as their teacher. And then when I was talking to Shiveya again, I could only hear her voice. I couldn't see her in form anymore. And she told me that the years ahead would be filled with many more struggles, and she would stay with me and I'll be strong enough to handle them, and not to forget that. And these two blond Amazonian-looking students of hers, which now I guess is my future self, the guy anyway — long, gorgeous hair, beautiful person, beautiful face, beautiful body, very ripped kind of abs. I was noticing the legs too, very hot. But he was wearing very ancient, very leather kind of clothes and he had a shield and a sword.

JOHN: Sort of a warrior.

BROUGH: But they were of peace; they would never use their weapons. And it was just a symbol of them being on a mission, I guess.

Anyway, they told me a lot of stuff and then I woke up from that, and I was like, "Oh, that was a profound one." And I still haven't forgotten it, fifteen years later.

JOHN: It's interesting because I had the impression before — we both did — that it was a kind of a new entity that had taken sight of us, and thought, "Hey."

BROUGH: Plucked us out of the crowd.

JOHN: I mean we knew it didn't just begin three months ago, but I didn't know that it was involved in your family history and all this stuff.

BROUGH: Only after that initial dream, and I guess the appearance of that Indian boy, which I haven't thought of in years — that wasn't like my normal psychic visions. I saw him clear as day. And he was just this beautiful-looking Indian boy with this robe.

JOHN: Which vision was this?

BROUGH: This was before I met Shiveya; this was the vision of this boy in a robe. And he was wearing traditional temple attire, which at the time I didn't know about. But now I know more about traditional Indian attire because I met an Indian person and I've heard about this. So, it's like okay, wow, he's in the troupe. And was almost respecting me, as if he knew that I was somehow advanced or something. I got that impression from him that day. Like he was, like, there for me, as if I was part of the light. Very weird.

Then I just put these things out of my head. Then my dad had those apparitions, which were directly related to my mom before she died. It was almost like an attempt — my dad has never had any strange paranormal experiences to that degree before that or after my mom's death. It was, like, two or three years before she passed.

JOHN: So, he came to you and told you about this.

BROUGH: My dad came to me that night. I was still awake, on my computer in my bedroom. And he opened my door and he goes,

"Have you been doing readings tonight?" And I was like, "What are you talking about?" And he looked really spooked, and he's like, "I had a ghost in my room." And apparently it's not a ghost at all.

JOHN: And it was going to try to change the timeline.

BROUGH: Mm-hm. It could very well have opened dialogue with my dad. Dad could have been like Gary Renard, having one of these things talk to him.

JOHN: And it would have maybe given him some kind of warning.

BROUGH: Mm-hm.

JOHN: I see. And they said it was frightening for him.

BROUGH: Yeah. Well, he told me that. So that's not news to me. It said one word to him. And he didn't tell me what that word was until after my mom died.

JOHN: What did he tell you?

BROUGH: He said, "Son" — and this is how annoying my father is — "Son, it told me a word, and that word changes everything. It has an effect on everyone."

"Dad, what's the word?"

"Oh, I can't tell you."

Why would he tell me that it said something if he wasn't going to give me the information? Why would he even do that?

JOHN: [*Laughing.*] It's like it's something out of *X-Files* or something.

BROUGH: So, after my mom died, I revisited the idea. I said, "So what was the word?" And my dad said that this was like the fourth or fifth appearance it made to him. It walked up to his bedside; this was the closest it had been to him.

JOHN: Was this all in the same night?

BROUGH: No — this was over a year or a couple years. My mother saw it once. So, this time it comes to his bedside, and it's right there, and he can see it, physically real. He could hear the footsteps, everything. It had long blond hair, tied up.

And the one word it said was "Dad."

And my dad said, "Fuck off!" And it disappeared.

JOHN: Dad. Meaning it was you.

BROUGH: But — my dad thinks it was the child my mother aborted between my older sister and me, which I only found out about after she died. She didn't want to tell me.

JOHN: But that's not what it was.

BROUGH: No. In fact — it was that — because I am the child. I reincarnated right after they tried to abort me.

JOHN: Wait — how did you figure that part out — you've learned that since then?

BROUGH: I had a psychic vision about it, yeah. My eyes — you know how I had eye surgery when I was a kid? I was mutilated — my soul had some memory from the abortion. So, I came in a little bit scrambled.

JOHN: I didn't know you had surgery.

BROUGH: Yeah, my eyes were profoundly crooked and all these things. So, I have a few genetic things. That also — to further what we were talking about, about forgiving my father this morning — he had pushed her into the abortion. And on some soul level I had bitterness toward him.

JOHN: Which explains a little more on the issues we were talking about earlier. Wow, this is really profound. I had no idea about any of that. So that was the word.

BROUGH: "Dad" was the word. So, he thought it was my brother. But I'm the reincarnation. So, it is me.

JOHN: You're your own bro.

BROUGH: Bro of the Brough.

Easter. It warned us! It said Easter. The resurrection.

JOHN: Wow. I didn't know today was going to be like this.

But it was saying, this orbit thing. Like we orbit around it.

BROUGH: We share a connection somehow.

JOHN: I've been wondering about this. That means you and I are both orbiting around the same—

BROUGH: Yeah, we're in a family.

Why don't we have a glass of wine and go to the roof?

[*While on the rooftop patio, we discuss the idea of whether the Voice was claiming to be the Indian god Shiva, with a slightly altered name. Later we have another session where we try to talk to Laron.*]

BROUGH: She seems present. She makes me feel like she was aware of what we did. I almost feel like she gives us a little congratulations, like a pat on the back.

I want to ask her what she thinks the identity of this being is, if she knew about this already, what she thinks about it.

She says, it's definitely a higher being. She's showing me. It's almost like, when they interact with it on their side, it can appear to them and then go back to where it came from, like, in a higher place. She wants to remind us that she doesn't want us to get lost in translation. It's already told us it's not a god.

It's that human interpretation, and the lore and the myth around this particular teacher is to make it a god, but it's not a god. A very advanced, very high being. I feel like Laron believes it. I'm a little torn. But Laron believes. She seems to be giving the A-okay. Like, I get a green light.

JOHN: So, Laron believes that the being is who she's claiming to be. In the sense of that particular historical figure of Shiva.

BROUGH: Yeah. She said to keep the focus on the content, not on the frame.

JOHN: *Ha ha.* Yeah, I like that.

BROUGH: And she wants to point out that as long as the information is consistent and helpful, it really doesn't necessarily matter if you believe who the entity is.

JOHN: Like I say, whether or not you think the proof is in the pudding, you still have the pudding.

BROUGH: Right. It's still Jell-O pudding. Instant oatmeal. But Laron's making me feel that it's trustworthy. She's surprised that I don't feel more proud to be discovering an aspect of my divine heritage. But I think that the higher being itself called it, in the sense that it's gonna take me some time to digest.

I kind of like the idea of, like, the Himalayas and India and stuff in the sense that it's not a place that I think of very often, and anyway why are spirits always Native American, you know what I mean? Why are they always Americans and Canadians and British people named Timmy and William? Like, why wouldn't there be all kinds of cultural — [*Brough goes for a moment into an imitation of Timmy, the young British boy with a Cockney accent who comes through in David Thompson channellings.*] Yeah, I find that makes it more believable in a sense, to me personally, 'cause it's not some...

She says, she's making me feel, like, as we develop, there's gonna be more of a relationship, more things will come to light. And just to take it step by step and keep going; we've been doing a good job. There will be a break at some point for us to properly work on the manuscript, and we'll be warned of it or we'll know when that happens. And that's when I can take more of an active role in the writing 'cause I'll have commentary to put things like this and help organize and structure. Yeah, that's what she makes me feel.

Do you have a question or anything for her?

JOHN: No, I think learning the specific identity is interesting because we can actually talk about history and learn some things about what gods mean in terms of mythology and religion.

BROUGH: Yeah, exactly, yeah.

JOHN: And already — I guess I'll say "she" — has said that, has revealed this information about her actually being female and rewritten as male, and that in itself is an interesting thing to hear.

BROUGH: Laron says that, not to get too lost in gender with it because its last life incarnation was as a she. It can appear as male or female. And could, and maybe will, appear to us in some form, at some point down the road, if it would be helpful. There's a lot that it can do. But it has chosen to remain distant, in the sense, like coming through in this form because it keeps the focus on the message.

Laron's like, it's normal to be skeptical and to be unsure of the origin of the information. But remember that bad trees can't produce good fruit.

JOHN: Again, I don't think the name or the identity is primary, because it's the content. So it could say, I'm Kermit the Frog, and really it's the content that matters, I agree with that. But it does help provide some kind of context as to where it's coming from. If we learned a little bit about the history, if it's had previous interactions with Earth, that's a good thing to know about. In the same sense that you learn really about anybody that you're talking to.

BROUGH: Right.

I was expecting it to be Fufu.

[*Referring to a female singing voice on one of John's ITC clips.*]

JOHN: Oh yeah. Starts making you sing.

Do you remember that time my ceiling fan was turning — did I do that, or did they do that…

BROUGH: It was your spirit guide.

JOHN: Okay. And then when that cutlery tray crashed down the other day?

BROUGH: She doesn't have access to information on that at this time. She can check into it for you though.

JOHN: Um, it's not that important, but sure.

What was Laron doing when you called on her? Was she doing something?

BROUGH: Yeah, well, she wasn't, um, she wasn't linked up with me, at that moment. She may have been with somebody.

JOHN: Does she have a sense of time that's similar to us? In that, does she have some kind of, like, day and night?

BROUGH: Yeah, well spirit guides, for the duration of our life on Earth, they choose to stay close to the Earth plane, so they're closer to our time, yeah.

But she has friends and people and things that she interacts with.

JOHN: Has she ever told you much about what she does and where she lives, her surroundings?

BROUGH: No, not too much. That could change; they could tell me more.

JOHN: What if you ask her?

[*Pause.*]

BROUGH: Well, she's very busy with regards to the readings. And she has friends and colleagues who she'll spend time with. And then

I see almost like a little place, a house or something, a home that she has, where her family can come down from higher realms and see her and visit. And studying, researching. There's a hall of records or some kind of a great hall, where she can access information. It's holographically ... She's busy. It's like a train station.

JOHN: Does she sleep or have some form of sleep?

BROUGH: Not required.

JOHN: And when you call on her, she just senses that and tunes into you?

BROUGH: Yes, there's a link.

JOHN: Is it a bit like just receiving a phone call or something and answering?

BROUGH: It's like when you think of someone you haven't seen in a long time and then you run across them the next day or they call. Magnify that phenomenon by a hundred. So, it's almost like a knowing that the person needs you.

But she's just basically saying, "You're doing great, keep it up."

[*EVP of female singsong voice, something like "won't back down."*]

Yeah, just wanted to see if I could link with her, just to find out what she thought of this. Yeah. I need time to digest. No farting around anymore here.

The Ancient Art of True Blessing

We attempted to channel on the night of March 31, but without much success. This could have been due to various factors — I hadn't yet finished transcribing the last session, and they may have been conscious of giving us more material too soon, creating a backlog. Also, Brough had been woken up early by a fire alarm in the building, which may have affected his state of mind. On top of all that, Brough was feeling that there was some kind of interference going on.

"In case we have interfering spirits," he said to me, "we've gotta take a walk and clear the space. I've had this in readings on occasion." We walked for a while, then resumed at 10:00 p.m., but nothing was happening. The door to the balcony was open and rain could be heard coming down.

BROUGH: I honestly don't know what's going on. It could just be that they're planning something.

JOHN: Hm. I thought they really wanted me to come over tonight. I don't know.

BROUGH: I really wanted to do this. All day I was telling my friends I was going to do this. I changed appointments.

JOHN: I feel like my state of mind's pretty wacky. It could be affecting things.

BROUGH: You're not the only one; mine is too. But is it wacky because—

JOHN: It almost feels like it's coming from them a bit.

BROUGH: They're not wanting to link. I don't think that we can really let them down. I think we're the passive instruments. I don't think that we tap into them and then we're blocking them. They might actually feel like they don't want us overlapping too much.

JOHN: Too soon after the last one you mean?

BROUGH: Well — got to finish writing the last one and all that. And maybe I still need to process.

JOHN: Well, even so, maybe they just wanted us to get together anyway.

[*Nineteen minutes in.*]

BROUGH: I'm right at the gate. I'm right where a voice could come through.

[*A rumble of thunder is heard.*]

Oh, okay. I just got a thought transmission. Their next project or teaching is to be something about a tool that can be used for dealing with death. Everyday situations in your life. It's very involved, it's gonna be a session, and they don't want to bring it through until we're finished going through the last one. And they, frankly, they're saying that the energy isn't there as much tonight to take on the task that they want to.

JOHN: Is that the energy from our side or their side?

BROUGH: No, it's our side. It's me. I'm probably tired. 'Cause the fire alarm this morning.

JOHN: Yeah. So the next one is quite involved?

BROUGH: Yeah, it's a big one, we got a doozy coming. They might cover it in two parts. Where we might have a break.

JOHN: So, we'll make sure we have a big chunk of time for that.

BROUGH: Yeah. Shiveya wants to make it so that it could be the last chunk of real substance for the first book. And we could start on the book after this next session.

JOHN: Wow. Yeah, that's my feeling, that we're going to have enough material soon.

BROUGH: I feel like she's giving us — "Good job for keeping committed" — a pat on the back or commendations for being committed to this. And that our goofy moods are our souls' expression that we get the night off, like we can play. But it's funny how we have many layers to us, like both of us intentionally want to be doing the channelling, but our souls on another level are like, "Okay, well, teacher doesn't need us."

Yeah, they're telling me we're in for a big number next session. Because it's gonna be challenging in the sense that, they're telling me we're going to be doing another exercise to further the meditation. And it's gonna be teaching some mental techniques. They're telling me that I will later on write an astral-projection development thing. [*Thunder.*] And that could even be a chapter. That might not even be for this book though. And possibly some predictions or something special that I don't know about.

And then we can begin organizing the material, categorizing everything that we've written and structuring it, like you said. And once we have some structure we'll be able to know what kinds of stories we want to put where.

But I just heard that she's proud of us.

JOHN: I'm curious to know more about her history on Earth as well. Is she able to say if we were correct about the historical figure of Shiva being her actual identity when on Earth?

[*Pause.*]

BROUGH: Although it doesn't matter, yes, that is the correct interpretation. I just heard, "There's time enough. All in good time. You'll find out more all in good time." Because she doesn't want to make it — like she doesn't even identify as a *she*. And it's already an example of how people are going to be prone to start taking it too literally. She doesn't want it to be on form, she wants it to be on content. And she's not upset that we're calling her "she," but that's an example.

JOHN: I just can't — to say "it" — "it" does not denote a conscious entity.

BROUGH: Yeah. And I would just say "Shiveya." Just use the name. [*This, however, forgets why we have pronouns to begin with — or we end up with "Shiveya says that Shiveya will talk about a topic that Shiveya thinks is very important…"*]

JOHN: Do you have an idea for when would be a good time to do the next one?

BROUGH: Oh. Oh, it's not about *when*, it's about the energy. We have to put some mind behind how we feel.

JOHN: Yes, okay. So, we'll tidy up the last one. And make sure we find a good time to do it.

* * *

We got to the next session three weeks later. It would have happened sooner, but I got sick and we had a mix-up about dates.

I started to get a feeling for when we were going to have a successful contact or not. Before a productive session, I felt a sense of fullness, like we had stored up enough time and energy, and something was due to come through.

We got together on the morning of April 23, 2016. A Saturday. The usual wacky mood took hold as contact approached. Within a few minutes of us taking our positions, Brough started to channel.

SHIVEYA: And what a pleasure it is to know you, be acquainted with you. Harbingers of laughter and joy. Although what is most amusing to me is how much fun the two of you can have out of nothing at all. Although I suppose it is better that you are making fun of nothingness than someone else.

How are you?

JOHN: I'm doing very well, thanks. It's great to talk to you.

SHIVEYA: Yes, we decided it would probably be best to allow Brough some time to adjust to the information from last session, but as well for you to process and transcribe it.

JOHN: And I got sick for a bit too.

SHIVEYA: Mm-hm. We wish to clarify — the work that we do can only enhance health; it does not take from it or subtract. Rather than thinking of yourselves as batteries, which could be drained, it would be more accurate to think of yourselves as light bulbs; when energy is passed through you, you light up.

Although it is possible, to that end, that you can be burnt out by a surge of too much energy. But we are what you might call "professional"; we do know exactly what we are doing. We would never burn you out.

JOHN: No, well I don't think I was sick from anything to do with this, that's for sure. It was just … life.

SHIVEYA: Yes — but you'll see on paper — I had to clarify that because the reader may have made that assumption.

Today there are a number of things that I wish to convey. Not the least of which, we will focus on practical exercises that can be done at the level of mind. And perhaps if you are willing and there is time, we will talk about any given subject that you wish to discuss that has been on your mind.

BROUGH: I'm just going to wait to see what they want to … Oh, I feel like it's gonna be a doozy. It's as if it's organizing its thoughts so that I can access them.

[*Shiveya then proceeds to deliver the following exercise.*]

Exercise

This practical exercise today falls into a two-step process, which must be always completed in the same order for reasons which I can explain later. This process, or exercise, is aimed at not only increasing your own vibrations closer to the higher vibration of love and further away from fear, but it is also aimed at restructuring the cognitive functions of your mind right down to the molecular level within your physical brain. Practising this daily will have profound consequences in the most positive of ways. It is a release, of sorts.

Start as always by sitting comfortably or lying down flat on your back, in a position or a chair that will support your entire body so that you may release all muscle control to the best of your abilities, consciously. Start by visualizing, with your eyes closed, the room that you are lying in filling with white light — pure, pristine, and shimmering.

And as that white light begins to surround you, the room actually begins to fade, almost as if it were a piece of photographic film fading out of existence until all that is left is a perfect white light. And you are at the centre of it.

If you can, visualize the street outside of this building or place around you. Visualize now that also fading into perfect white light until all that is left is the white. Now, expand to the city, to the continent, to the world. All the way up to the stars, space, the galaxy, all the galaxies. And begin to see that image fade until all that is left is white light. And now you find yourself the single point in the midst of this vast continuum of perfect continuity, white light.

And suddenly, before you appears an altar. Perhaps it is a plank of wood or a marble table, whichever you wish your altar to be. And for a moment, access your thoughts, access the thing that is stressing you or that you find disturbs your peace most frequently.

It might be a symbol of money, currency, work. It might be an individual from your past who is no longer in your life, someone who has died or with whom you have been through a painful or infuriating separation, for example. Maybe someone who is in your present; a nuisance, a person who triggers you.

You can either place the object on that altar, sitting there looking contented, or if this is a person, I encourage you to kneel before the altar with them, either hand in hand or kneeling beside each other.

And now, the altar begins to fade to white light. But this time as it does, access your thoughts once again and consciously think about the experience of surrendering, giving up, as it were.

Give the thing, the person, or the situation that is most disturbing, up to the light. As it fades and is now completely gone, there is nothing but total light.

And to your surprise, your own body begins to fade and become more and more translucent, until suddenly at that final moment before your body is completely gone, you become aware that you never were and never could be a body, that you indeed are the light, one with it forever, and always extending in every direction without any borders, any boundaries, any limits. Farther than even the known reaches of the universe.

And everyone or everything that you could ever want or need is already part of you, provided for you. No enemies, no separations; just total, whole, and perfect.

And in this state of total oneness — having released the person or situation or object that you have found yourself either yearning for to the point of disturbance or pining after to the point of nuisance or bother — it [*the thing you released*] is now completely surrendered to a much larger version of yourself. A version of yourself that, dare I say, is pure spirit and that operates with infinite intelligence and can find a solution to any situation. For this is you accessing your higher mind.

This is the true meaning of forgiveness, which is to say that you should give everything up to higher reason rather than subject it to your own infinitesimally small agenda.

And in this state, it is useful to access the memory or experience of gratitude. This is the final step to this meditation. As you exist as pure infinite expansion — one with all, impossible to separate — be grateful. Grateful that everything you ever needed or wanted is there and can be provided for you. And that all wars have come to an end, forever. And that you are one with the master vibration; what you might even call "God," for those of you who are more religiously inclined.

And after you have existed for a time in this state, slowly bring yourself back to the world where you think that you are. You will notice a feeling of increased relaxation at first, when operating and practising this.

But in time, with further practice, several things will begin to happen, first of which is an increase in synchronistic events. You will also notice at the periphery of your vision, flashes and sparks of light. This light phenomenon also ties into the synchronicities. And ultimately you will also notice you become far less irritable.

The goal of this teaching is to learn to be able to practise it mentally on the spot in situations where you are irritated, without having to lie down or meditate or close your eyes. To instantly visualize whomever or whatever it is and yourself both fading into white light and a feeling of surrender, giving it up to higher consciousness. Knowing perfectly well that answers will begin to come to you out of the blue without much cognitive functioning on your own.

Carrying forth that practice on a daily basis will undo decades of neural programming which you have inflicted on yourselves. Your particular triggers, your particular reactions, things that bother you, your preferences — all of which can be undone. They were, after all, learned behaviours in the first place. And what has been learned can be unlearned. *And some things that have been learned should be unlearned. And replaced with a healthier modality.*

For the second phase — please remember that this phase should always be practised after the first phase, never before, because the second phase has powerful consequences, and if used improperly can result in devastating outcomes. After all, it was once said, a consciously guided miracle is often something that can yield devastating results.

This secondary part of the practice is particularly useful when the subject of your surrender happens to be a person. After you have joined with spirit and surrendered that thing, now you are free to practise something, which we can call "the ancient forgotten art of true blessing." As Brough has been so fond of pointing out, in a humorous way, nobody truly seems to bless one another or wish one another well in this world anymore. Unless someone sneezes.

The ancient forgotten art of true blessing is a quite powerful one at that. And it goes as follows: Once in a completely objective and calm state of mind, achieved through forgiveness, take a moment to access your thoughts about an individual; the individual you have forgiven, that is. And begin to see their life.

And begin to visualize for them — ask for guidance on this from spirit — the most wonderful life that you can muster in your mind. It is important that while you do this, you do not use any logic, you do not put any limits, you do not enforce what you think would be good for the person.

But rather, take some time and use detailed imagery to visualize a life filled with the best health, the best friendships, the best love, the best food, the best money, the best lifestyle — perhaps even better than you've ever had yourself. Dare I say it, perhaps even better than you ever will have. Give it all to them without any boundaries or limitations. See their life filled with laughter, wonderful physicality, joy.

At first, if you are doing this correctly, the ego remnants in your subconscious mind will have resistance. You should feel slightly irritated that this person should have more than you or better than you. That is a good sign that you are doing good work. You always want to rattle the ego.

Eventually, and with enough practice, you should start to feel elation and excitement at the gifts that you give. After you've taken some time to focus acutely, with detail, an absolutely wonderful and marvellous life for this other person, you now must remember and take note that, for some mysterious reason during this practice, you did not visualize yourself in that person's life. That's not a mistake — you see, you are operating from a place of superposition. You are spirit. And you are finally using your thoughts correctly; perhaps for the first time in your lifetime. And hopefully not for the last.

For every thought form that you send out, blessing another with a perfect life, you have begun to magnetize toward yourself every single blessing that you have given. For the gifts you give are kept safe for you by spirit. It is a two-way street, my friends.

And so, the first step is to surrender your judgements and your ideas and agendas, in the form of a person or a vision. And then, the second phase is to short-circuit the karmic cycle by sending out only love, in its total and perfect form from the superposition of ultimate spirit. For you have begun your journey on the wonderful playground of becoming a master.

Those of you who have the insight and wisdom to continue with this practice and to use it daily will accelerate your spiritual growth by leaps and bounds. For as Brough likes to say, you will have catapulted yourself light-years ahead. Perhaps faster than any yogic class or dietary preference or political belief that you think you have.

To go back to something that I had mentioned about phase one of the practice: The reason synchronicities will start to occur after you have operated with forgiveness and surrender is because you will have begun to undo karma itself. For it is karma, it is the old script, the usual humdrum, that would have you react to another person who you perceive to have wronged you, by throwing guilt at them and making them feel that they have done wrong.

If you can resist the temptation to show someone or tell someone that they are wrong and instead surrender to spirit immediately, what you have done is interrupted your regularly scheduled thought programming. For now you have started to do something new and unusual, which is to step outside of conflict altogether. This is a simple procedure but a very difficult one indeed. Especially when you are in a body, and you have carnal urges.

But when you do this, the thought forms that now shine down from your higher self will literally begin to erase possible timelines that you would have lived and you no longer need, as you have learned your karmic lesson. You may not be conscious of having learned a lesson when you forgive a person, but suffice to say, all lessons lead to you learning to let go of your attachment to your ideas and your agenda in favour of the ideals and the script of a higher consciousness, a higher intelligence, that is your higher mind.

And when you embrace that higher mind, it finally can begin to work in your favour. And as great rays of beautiful shimmering light shine down through the universe of space and time, through dimensions, they begin to erase — much like the light replacing shadows — various negative experiences which you no longer need. The results of which cause the rivers and flowing timelines to begin to change and channel into one singular river, one singular cohesive timeline.

And it is when one channel meets another and submerges into one river — where you may be walking through your day and, because you were fifteen minutes late for some unknown reason, you cross paths with an old friend or an old love that you never had reconciliation with. And it is in that moment where you are overwhelmed with a feeling of wonderment and awe and excitement, and both of you seem to be elated.

Although you may have left each other on bad terms, you are given always another chance to rectify the situation. What would have taken a lifetime to find the other soul in a new body can happen in this lifetime. For there is never any goodbye — only "until next time"; I have said that before.

Through your spiritual practices, synchronicities will bring you back around to those who you need to find peace with, to have a chance to do things correctly once again. Another form of synchronicity will be symbols and signs, parallel coincidences, thinking of a thought, remembering a quote and then seeing it on a billboard or a sign or hearing it over the casual conversation of two people sitting in a café. Things of that nature.

All of synchronicity is a side effect of changes being made in the space-time continuum around you. Know that when you begin to see synchronicity, it is because your higher mind is erasing possible timelines, which you no longer need to learn your lessons. Both you — John — and Brough have noted many synchronicities over the years, and of course now is the time to inform you that it is because both of you have been accelerating in your spiritual advancement.

For when a person ceases to see synchronicity, it is indicative that they are stagnated in their spiritual growth. Indeed, when this book is published, you will notice that you receive many emails from people telling you about their synchronicities. It's important to remind them that the synchronicity itself is not always a profound message but simply a signpost, or an indication, that something is happening on their behalf at a much higher level.

As for the light anomalies — flashes, sparks that you will start to see as a result of this practice — that is you seeing through the physical world into the world of spirit. It is almost as if those lights represent pinpricks of light from your true home shining through into this world, which is of course a symbol of the great rays extending from your higher mind, washing away the unnecessary difficulties of karma, and creating a more cohesive timeline for your life.

For your mind, I have said, is very powerful, and if used correctly, you would be amazed at what you can do. Contemplate for a second, gentlemen, that you have power over time itself, but nobody has ever encouraged you or taught you how to use it.

Brough was reading your article recently, which you had published eight years ago, and there was a quote by a spirit gentleman in the astral realm explaining the purpose of ITC. Brough took special note of a mysterious expression that very few people would understand, at the end of his quote, which was, "It is ours to master time." Indeed, is this not what he was tuning in to?

The Origins of Guilt

A few days later we had a short session with someone else there for the first time. Brough's friend Baz was visiting. I was unsure of having someone else there, as we'd never included another person before (apart from Charles dropping in towards the end of the first session), and Baz and I hadn't even met. Brough and I talked about it and decided we could give it a try with him there. Baz (short for Basil) was a very nice guy, and we hung out a bit and did some barbeque on the roof before the session. I felt comfortable having him there.

As usual, we got into the crazy joking mood, and Baz joined in. We talked about people in older times having pillows full of bacteria and growing cheese on them. Often our humour involved strange, exaggerated takes on life in the Victorian era. I felt that with three of us there, this comedy routine could go on for a while, so I asked the boys to settle down in hopes that we could start the channelling session. I didn't want to go too late on a work night.

In this session, Brough was asked to relate a story from high school to illustrate the theme introduced by Shiveya, involving the nature and causes of guilt.

BROUGH: Okay, I got contact. It's telling us not to worry, that the joking around is good because we're getting our minds on the same track, in case we haven't noticed.

Yeah, it doesn't matter what you joke and talk about, within reason. It can't be negative or detrimental, but you're getting on the same wavelength, which is what they need to know: how to get through into our wavelength. And not to feel that what we were doing is silly, it's actually quite intentional; we just didn't know it.

JOHN: I feel that way too. I feel that it gets us in the mood.

BROUGH: Not a mood — you were actually sensing it was about to come through.

JOHN: Well, we get giddy as it approaches. We consistently do that.

BROUGH: It appreciates the intention.

SHIVEYA: We appreciate your sincerity JT.

Let us pick up from where we left off. Would you move the recorder closer?

[*This is the first time the recorder is referred to. It is actually the usual distance. I move it closer. I wonder if they would be aware if it wasn't working, say, if the batteries ran out.*]

SHIVEYA: One moment please.

A very important topic that must be discussed is guilt.

It is not one often brought up in the New Age community or in many spiritual communities. However, we hear often about people who have near-death experiences, travelling through a tunnel and seeing the light and reuniting with their ancestors, seeing wonderful things.

In contrast to this, a very small minority of near-death experiencers feel quite left out because they experience hellish conditions. This is in fact a truth. For them it is confusing because there is no hell and yet they've experienced something awful — sometimes a vast expanse so great and so cold it is beyond words, where they find themselves completely isolated and alone.

They are thankful beyond words to be reunited and resuscitated back into their body, where they are forever transformed, knowing that there is something after death, however not something that they look forward to. For others, they experience something different than the great abyss: torment, frightening imagery, difficulty — darker, lower spheres.

These are states of mind, not places that you go. And the root cause is guilt. At the very beginning of this book, the beginning of these sessions, starting in October this last year, we addressed that spirit's function is to build bridges and bring union to separation itself. And now we address the true origin of separation: guilt.

And so seldom is this word used or even given any exploration, except of course in the hands of manipulative people. "Guilt" is not a bad word; ironically, it is nothing to feel guilty for. Rather it is a mental construct, a weapon that you have invented to enslave yourselves. And as with any great war where weapons of mass destruction are implemented, it takes nothing less than genius to undo and bring reparation to the devastating consequences of such deeds.

You are infinite. Contemplate that for one moment. There is nothing beyond your reach. Absolutely nothing. It is only the illusion of spatial time which makes you think that there are things beyond you. Of course, once you are beyond this body, you will realize, slowly but surely, that this is not so.

And yet, you make believe that you have somehow fractured off from, separated from, the great whole and become isolated and individualistic and unique. And you are going to now venture off and do it better than before, often forgetting where you came from.

But of course, you feel guilty without even knowing it, that you have turned your back on the whole, your brothers and sisters. Some of you might even use "God" as a term. And because you have turned your back on this, the whole, in order to become one, you carry with you a sense of responsibility for the whole, rather ironically. That sense of responsibility translates directly into guilt.

Guilt, meaning you hold and bear the burden of the feelings of others and the state of others. It is a truly advanced being who knows what to do with guilt. "Guilt" is not a bad word, I'll say again; it is not a curse, although it leads to every ill consequence that you can imagine. Which is why it is your job to refuse to take on guilt from others — especially when they wish it upon you.

This, however, is not a permission slip to cause harm and then tell people that you're not to blame. In fact, if you've read the book so far, you know that your task is to cause relief and bring love, laughter, and peace everywhere you go. You will fail, but luckily, you have eternity to get it right.

And where guilt is concerned, it is no longer your friend or ally. Holding guilt does not make you more worthy. Admitting that you were wrong before others can point it out does not somehow make you more intelligent. For that is an illusion.

For it is your task to learn how to undo guilt until there is nothing left but love and laughter. This is only accomplished through a mixture of life experience leading to self-actualization, which could also be coined a "psycho-education," which is to familiarize yourself with the workings of the mind and spirit.

This is followed by an implementation or an active process or spiritual activity — spiritual activity being to use your thinking properly. Rather than thinking that thoughts happen to you, take control of them and use them for your own accord. With the aim of love, forgiveness, and truth.

We've talked about how to forgive — about visualization of surrender, and then the great forgotten gift of blessing. This will come in handy and be quite a fun practice for many. And as you practise these techniques, you will notice that your guilt diminishes. In fact, oftentimes after practising this technique, you will find that you notice when people project their guilt. And it will be hilarious to you.

It's appropriate to recall one of Brough's personal experiences from high school.

BROUGH: Oh no ... [*Laughing.*] ... oh God. No please don't. Not this one! Okay!

JOHN: Yeah, you sure?

BROUGH: Yeah ... it's telling me ... okay...

I was in the cafeteria and there was this kid named Eric and he was in a motorized wheelchair.

And he ran over my foot in the wheelchair, then turned around and looked at me and said, "Watch where you're going, idiot!"

I didn't say anything, but I was like, "You ran *me* over. I was just standing here in line for food and you ran *me* over."

JOHN: So, what does that have to do with guilt?

BROUGH: That's the example. That's the projection of guilt.

JOHN: He projected guilt onto you.

BROUGH: He projected his guilt from him not watching where he was going, so it was my fault, and then — I actually felt horrible because he was in a wheelchair.

JOHN: Right, you were the bad guy.

BROUGH: So, it was a guilt fest — everyone was bad, we're just all bad people, there was no fixing the situation. And almost like, the thing about Eric — and I'm having an *ah-ha* moment right now — as I leaned in to go and help him, he, like, turned his wheelchair — *zzzz!* — like, gave me the cold shoulder by turning the joystick, like nothing I could do would make it better, like guilt was the end. And we imprisoned ourselves. There was no way to fix it.

[*Pause.*]

SHIVEYA: Not quite the way spirit would have worded it. But that gets the point across.

That's an excellent example of what people do with their guilt. Had Brough been at the state he is at now, he would have laughed more readily in the moment and indeed seen it for what it was — a call for love in his brother. For those who project guilt are those who are suffering.

Those who do good, feel good within, first. We've said this earlier. Those who do bad, feel bad inside of themselves first. Feelings and thoughts come first, actions always follow; it is not the other way around.

That however does not discount surprises. It's possible to be walking along feeling wonderful only to be met with a surprise. But with every surprise comes a choice of how you want to feel. And when the surprise is, quote unquote, unpleasant, you can forgive. You can use it for the right reason and suddenly transform the situation into an opportunity for peace.

To Brough's credit, there are people who would have bullied or pushed or said something under their breath to Eric in the wheelchair. But Brough did maintain his composure, and although he felt terrible, he turned and said nothing. Sometimes to do no harm is all you can do. To remain frozen is all you can do.

Guilt comes from an ancient memory that you have forgotten. Now there are some people reading the book who will feel that they can remember anything they want to. This is not so. Your mind is far more complex, abstract, and deep than you can personally and intentionally access.

You may disagree, and that is fine; that's your wish. Although you are insulting yourself if you think that in your current form you are the penultimate, and that you can access anything you want. For indeed if this is what you think the highest form is, then here is where you shall stay.

The truth is, you are much vaster than your physical experience dictates and can ever dictate. And the source of guilt comes from a time before measurable time, before physicality itself, before the dimensions of the measurable universe. It came from the instant that you forgot that you are one with all.

And so, on your journey home — and this is the only metaphor that we use in this chapter — not your journey to physical death but the journey to life, to awakening, to understanding, if you wish to truly feel and experience oneness, you must use the forgiveness technique. This is not a new teaching, but it is a seldom-used one.

Keep in mind the subject of this particular manuscript is that of *relationships*. There is a depth and scope that will tie into world affairs, that will tie into the future of humanity, that will tie into technological advancements, as well as spiritual development, in terms of psychical abilities and out-of-body experiences — various other subjects in books to come.

Know that we are proud. Know that for us, you are but one fraction, one fragment of the whole, and without you, we are nothing, and vice versa. For it is only in joining and the coming together of minds that we can truly accomplish any great feat. Indeed, look at any tall structure in your world.

[*I am fixed visually on the CN Tower, visible from Brough's apartment, as he speaks.*]

This was not done by any one man or woman. And as you come together in the spirit of love and laugher and peace, great things will be accomplished.

For tonight I will leave you with something Brough is fond of: how easy it is to break down, and how much energy and effort it takes to build up.

Much love.

[*Pause.*]

BROUGH: I think it was a finishing-up of the last session. My impression was it was to be taken as part of the last thing, the last one we did.

JOHN: The last one, which was about forgiveness.

BROUGH: I feel that they're one thing; it's a unit.

[*In the last session, they left the option open to continue later in the day — this may be what will come through if we continue.*]

BROUGH: Usually it goes on longer than this, and it's a little more casual, like it talks to us, and it lets us ask questions.

JOHN: It's pretty open-ended. Tonight may be just a time constraint in terms of me getting to bed and going to work.

BROUGH: My heart rate shot up too. I thought that was really weird.

But you know — I just got this now — the subject of guilt is inherent, on a very spiritual, deep level, and it's difficult to confront. And how to deal with it and what it really means is controversial to the ego. And whether we are conscious of it or not, our egos are flaring up, and that could get in the way. So, it's Shiveya trying to send a laser beam through, before it gets — *shhht!* — cut off.

So, it's not that it's cutting us off, it's that the ego cuts it off. That's what we're not getting. That's why my heart rate — like if you take my pulse — when we confront something that is difficult to handle, it's going to come across — because it is a being of love — it's going to come across in ways that we can handle, and dare I say it, even if we think that we can handle it, if we write it out then we're thinking about it, then we deal with it, so when it comes across in the manuscript, the reader will handle it better.

Because we are now given the time to really process this properly.

JOHN: Well, it's odd because I had a situation involving someone in a wheelchair today.

BROUGH: What happened?

JOHN: It wasn't quite like your situation, but I was helping with this event, and there were, like, twenty people coming, and we could only get a room that would fit ten or something, and we were just squishing everyone in. So I run off to get more chairs and there's a man in a wheelchair, like, he has stuck himself into the doorway, like, everyone's already stuffed in and I'm trying to stuff more people in, and he has come in with his wheelchair, which I didn't blame him for, but I was like, "Oh shit," after everyone else is stuffed in, he was in the doorway, and more people are still trying to come in.

BROUGH: And that's the same day.

JOHN: This was just today. This afternoon.

BROUGH: Okay, that's interesting. That's always happening to us, Baz, with the analogies and things.

JOHN: But he didn't — there was no intention like that on his part.

BROUGH: No, no, no — but at the same time, he had to be, on some level, aware that it's a small room and there could be extra people coming, and his entitlement that "I'm in a wheelchair and therefore I deserve…"

JOHN: Oh, I don't know—

BROUGH: There's the guilt — no, no, no, no! [*Voice very raised.*] It's not conscious but it's the guilt, that's what you're not understanding. This is what I'm trying to say is cutting us off, it's that — and then the making excuses — it's that there has to be some self-awareness that he is in the door with his wheelchair and it's a small space, and it's not that he's trying, it's not that he's mad, it's none of that, it's the, "I'm just not going to care about this."

But then secretly he has the guilt. Secretly he does. 'Cause he's self-aware. But he's entitled. But then — but it's not even a thing, it's so stupid! All of it is so stupid, the guilt is not necessary. But it's there.

And that's what's being — I don't understand, I don't have the words for it. But that's what I'm saying. And what do you do with that stuff that you can't help but notice.

JOHN: But who's got the guilt in that situation. Do I have it, or does he have it, or both?

BROUGH: Well — first of all — I know about the space that I take up in this world. And I don't know how I know this, but I've always been extremely gracious as a person. I've always been able to step out of the way, and I've tended to make so much space for everybody that sometimes I even exclude myself, and I don't take my space enough.

And some people just take their space too much. And it's all the same thing but from two sides of the same coin. Me, I don't feel worthy enough, and they feel too worthy. And people just don't — just get rid of the guilt, then just — "Hold on, let's be logical, I need to be the last one into this, let me make sure I make room for everyone else at the meeting because I'm the one who's going to come in last and leave first … blah blah blah blah blah…" But with the guilt, those rational decisions can't be made.

Without the guilt, finally those rational decisions can be made. Because people can just be, "Oh okay, that's how you feel, and that's where this belongs, and blah blah," but when you bring in the entitlement, and you bring in all the crap, all the human emotion is founded on guilt, and you can still have emotion and be human, but when you extricate the guilt, you're not doing foolish things, and people aren't in awkward situations anymore.

JOHN: Yes, that's right. You're just communicating more clearly.

BROUGH: Communication — exactly. And it's through, first of all, self, before you can communicate properly externally. It's like that.

JOHN: That's what I try to do, actually. 'Cause I realize a lot of conversations are filled with people saying, "Oh sorry," and expressing kind of their guilt, but let's stop with all the fucking sorry, and let's just talk about what we need to talk about. What are we trying to get across? And people constantly apologizing when they brush against you on the subway and shit like that, I'm just done with that. Like, the amount of sorry.

But isn't guilt in some way — this was going through my head during the talk — if guilt is what happens to you after you forget that you're part of the whole and you go off on your own, isn't guilt that thing that's then calling you back?

BROUGH: I think we're going to talk about that. Because I heard that too. I heard that that's where it's going to lead in another conversation. It's ironic that it's both purposeless because you can't be separate from the whole, but it's an indication of the fact that you love people.

Ironically, you project that you hate them and you blame them because you wish that you could be one with them so much. It's all just a convoluted thing. That's where it gets into the forgiveness part. Forgiveness allows you to actively treat this dynamic, of projection of guilt.

JOHN: If someone had committed a heinous crime, and then in prison later on they started to gradually feel remorse, wouldn't that be an indication that they still have a chance of redemption because they feel the pain of what they've done?

BROUGH: That's a great question. You know me — I don't believe in hell. I think this is hell 'cause, technically, this is the only place in the universe where you could actually physically be burned alive. I mean once you're dead you can't be burned.

JOHN: Well, surely suffering exists in other parts of the—

BROUGH: Psychological suffering.

JOHN: Well, maybe this is all psychological suffering.

BROUGH: Right. Right! But burned alive?

JOHN: Well, you're talking about physical suffering.

BROUGH: But still, you're saying even physical suffering is mental. Which I agree with. But my point being that Shiveya brought up a period of suffering after death, which is not what we hear about commonly. And how there is a group of people who have had that and come back and feel very alone — because nobody addresses that, which is kind of neat, because our books can address that.

JOHN: In one of the books I have by — I can't remember her name [*I later remember it's P.M.H. Atwater*] — one of the big researchers in that area, she specifically gets into that.

BROUGH: Really. Okay. So, we're getting into that. It's bringing that up and it's talking about how guilt is the ultimate cause. And in previous sessions it's talked about how thought can create your realities, so—

JOHN: That's exactly what I've always thought about those experiences, was that it was from guilt.

BROUGH: You've always felt that?

JOHN: I already thought that, yes. I can't say I know it, but it made sense to me, that when someone has that experience it's because they're harbouring something, the idea that they deserved that.

BROUGH: They're punishing themselves.

JOHN: They deserve it! They're going to hell because they're supposed to go to hell.

BROUGH: Right, and I always thought — which I guess is the same thing — I always thought they were just stupid religious fundamentalists who just created this for themselves because they didn't feel worthy of heaven. Which is the same thing!

JOHN: Same thing. And maybe it's a tidy explanation, maybe it's a generalization, I don't know. But a lot of people see what they expect to see, right, so they expect to see Jesus if they're very Christian, and they end up seeing Jesus, and same for, you know, the other gods. And so, yeah, I feel there's some sense of self-persecution, maybe, that comes into play.

BROUGH: Right. And so the cure, according to this feeling I have tonight, is to implement a practice of forgiving each other and loving one another because, if what I think about you is secretly what I feel I deserve to get, then what I give to you is love, then I must deserve love. So it's almost like a trick. [*Claps hands.*] Like a cheat, like a code, like a hack! Like you're hacking the system, like the matrix.

So, if I can just give love all the time, then I deserve love. But not from you, necessarily, not love in the way that I want it. But just the fact that I'm a decent person. And that's why the mobsters who kill people, and on their deathbed ask for the Father to come and repent to, it doesn't work. 'Cause they're not really — they are guilty for all that shit.

[*We start imitating mobsters in a Godfather-like voice.*]

JOHN: I'm sorry!

BROUGH: Father, you married my daughter and you buried my son, who I killed in a mob accident.

JOHN: I just need a couple Hail Marys.

BAZ: So I can go to heaven.

BROUGH: Heaven would be at a great loss without me.

JOHN: I could really do them a lot of favours up there.

BROUGH: I've sent a lot of demons to hell for you guys. Jesus had nothing on me. Jesus couldn't survive in the Bronx.

So this whole concept of like — and it's not religiousness, it's not repentance, it's just awareness that you don't have to feel you fucked up. We make mistakes. We step on each other's toes, or in some cases, drive over them. But even still, it's not like Eric did that to me on purpose; it was just funny that he had to make it sound like I ... wasn't watching where I was going.

JOHN: Maybe he needed to maintain his position as the persecuted one.

BROUGH: That's it.

JOHN: So, in his logic, he couldn't bring himself to apologize, because then he's not the persecuted one.

BROUGH: Right, because if he took personal ownership of his action, he would have retained his personal power. But instead he stuck with the power of the motorized wheelchair, which ran over my foot.

JOHN: Which probably hurt like a son of a bitch.

BROUGH: It was surprisingly not that painful, 'cause I had Doc Martens on with steel toes.

The Duality of Progression and Regression

We convened on the night of May 20. We didn't know it at the time, but this session would conclude the first book. This would be another brief contact, but would beautifully deliver ideas about tendencies in people to embrace or resist growth.

BROUGH: It's like we've been connected all night, actually. Everything ties into something here. Everything we've talked about ties into the same theme.

SHIVEYA: As you know, tonight was meant to happen, as every night that you convene for these sessions is pre-scripted to a degree. And our thoughts are able to intertwine with yours and affect yours, as a sort of mental merging occurs between transmitter and recipient. Of course, the recipient must always be willing to some degree, or at least open-minded to receive.

There is a concept that must be addressed this evening. For it is a discovery that has not been yet made in your world, although when expressed here, it will seem so obvious and blatant as the sky is blue on a sunny day, one will wonder why one hasn't thought of it before.

For at the very beginning of these channellings, we explained to you the concept of duality. For the presence of light, or being, and the absence of, are caused by a fundamental conflict in the mind.

To hold true to our original point, duality appears everywhere in nature. Because all creatures in human and physical form are experiencing a profound split in their psyche at a very deep level. Where once you were only made of love, and now you are both love and fear.

Never at the same time, I might add. For it is impossible to be both love and fear at the same time. You simply oscillate between the two, unable to make up your minds, constantly in turmoil, cognitive dissonance, at levels you're not even conscious of. And this phenomenon expresses itself quite clearly within your civilization.

For just as there always seem to be wars and unending conflicts between peoples, there are many, many philosophers and theorists in society, luminaries who have theories as to how and why this exists, practical answers to overcome. And indeed the answers are bridging and beginning to break the surface to the conscious world, which of course is education. Education, awareness — to obtain knowledge is the cure for all conflict.

To strive for deeper states of knowing has to be the end of conflict because the closer to knowledge and truth that you get, you will inevitably realize that you and everything around you are a part of a whole. One organism, one mechanism. And that separation is simply an illusion.

Now, in this day and age in your world, there appears to be very strong polarity in the world. You can almost draw it on a map. Where once, between the British colonies that came to the Western world, there was a very clear divide between the mindsets of those who lived in the South and those who lived in the North. To make a perfect cross-section across the world now in the twenty-first century, there seems to be a divide between East and West in much the same way. And it is the same exact divide that has always occurred in history.

You see there are those in life who are ready for progress, to move forward, to make discoveries and shed habits and shed rituals and live in truth. And these are brave individuals and spiritually advanced individuals, because to live in truth sometimes requires that you change your mind. But then there are those for whom you could coin the term "regressionists": people who wish to stay the same as yesterday.

One of Brough's favourite sayings is that laughter is spoken the same in every language. Whatever beliefs you hold, or whichever culture you belong to, in wherever in the world you were raised, or whatever your problems may be, when you boil everything down to its core element, there are those beings who are afraid to move forward, and then there are those beings who are willing to move forward. For this is the source of all war and all conflict within your world.

Now, the great catch-22 is that, if you are spiritually advanced, you must know that it is forbidden to change another or to even attempt to change another's mind. And the more power you attain in your existence and the more ability you have to permeate and guide the thoughts of others, the minds of others, the more you must refrain from ever using your power to willfully change others.

Something we have been working on with Brough is that everything in its form, whether agreeable or not, is absolutely belonging. For those who are regressive, who are afraid to face the future, it is a temporary state. And it is a state of denial, as there is only one direction, and that direction is the road home.

We must have compassion for those who cling to archaic, religious, dogmatic belief and who use their twisted interpretations to cause harm and pain to others. The reason you must have compassion for these individuals is because their total fear is the fear of death. For, anyone who is a progressive, anyone who is a forward-thinking individual, they know that death occurs on many levels in this life, even before you are physically gone and shed your mortal coil.

For there is death of personality, birth of new forms and new ideas and new self-realization, and indeed the great irony is that in your world, the process of life involves constant death, and this is again a reflection of duality in the universe — that you can never have something without the other.

But why progressive people are spiritually evolved is because they are able to accept and embrace the irony. They are able to acknowledge their own regressive tendencies. Whereas those who remain in an unhealthy one-sided form of denial of regressiveness are incapable of grasping a larger scope, you see, so to that end, they are very narrow-minded.

This is not good or bad, as everything does belong, but it is important to acknowledge because there will come a time in human history, and it will be a very long time from this point in history, where civilization will become enlightened, and there will be no more regressives, no more people who are wishing for yesterday and clinging to the past. Rather everyone will come to a common consensus about what reality is. Your science and your technology and your art are not yet advanced enough for this epitome to be reached.

Another concept that's been addressed through these channellings, this project, is that your thoughts matter. It is important to look within yourself and seek out the areas of your psyche and thought patterns where you hold on to the past and you hold on to notions that hold you back from progress and growth.

And since growth is a part of nature, to do anything that attempts to countermand it is to be insane. You are resisting reality. And so it is healthy to challenge the things about yourself that resist progress, on any level: progress of ideas, progress of growth, progress of health. Not merely accomplishing personal goals, for there are many people who could be categorized as very regressive and yet they exercise, take care of themselves, are engaged in their communities.

The reason they remain regressive is that they are only engaged in their communities in a specific way that they deem valuable. That they have an ideology about what is useful and that they stick to only what their ideas entail, rather than being open-minded and learning to truly become useful by being able to adapt to the situations of the day.

Alas, no matter how slow someone's growth appears to be, it is never completely still, because one of the laws of nature is growth and change. Both yourself — John — and Brough are rapidly growing; you've seen it over the years of knowing each other. Death and rebirth of personality, change of relationship.

And naturally, your own relationships with others have grown and changed and come to endings, which has not always been easy. The road forward is not always one free of challenge. But as you will come to discover, through the guidance of spirit and your own personal braveries, that it is one that is very worth taking. For you are on the path to your truest and highest destinies. And all it requires is open-mindedness, a sense of humour, and a willingness, a very small willingness I might add, to experience the fruits of life.

Because this is how you are and this is how you've evolved to become, it is almost completely alien to you that there are those out there who would read these words and find them threatening and completely unappealing. As I stated, what I speak of here is so fundamentally true, one may ask oneself, "How come I've never thought that?"

It's obvious it's ingrained. From the beginning of this project, we've stated multiple times that the kinds of concepts being discussed are universal truths, which means they're true no matter what, all over, without question. Which is a concept that is completely threatening to those who want to personalize truth and separate further.

Brough has often pointed out that in the spiritual/New Age community, one of the more annoying phrases that people use is "That is not true for me," as if to suggest that truth can be divided, separated into small chunks, and that some pieces are more valuable than others. This is a mistaken concept by people in an early phase of spiritual development.

The truth remains the truth whether you know about it or not. And it is your job and responsibility to come to discover it. And you will discover it and rediscover it, and different levels, and understand it better as you go. For there is a part of you that understands it fully that cannot be expressed through your current physical form. And there is a part of you that comes into physical form in order to forget everything, so that you can remember it more wholly and from a better vantage point. This is a concept for another project, which will happen eventually. And that project will deal with the concept of why life occurs.

The true form of this book, as was discussed in a previous chapter, is to deal with relationship. And the common theme throughout the project is to suggest that your relationships with others can only be as good or as bad as your relationship with self. And the necessity to be completely open-minded and completely honest with yourself and to be able to have a sense of humour about yourself is necessary for you to have peace with others.

For to fail at this relationship with self, you will see erroneousness and errors throughout the rest of your life. Unfortunately, that is what is considered a normal life in your world at this time. There are those who seek for something better, an experience of reality that is congruent, consistent, and filled with mostly joy, although it can never be completely joyous in your world, and that's not without its own reasons and purpose. Again, that is a subject for another time.

You are very valuable to us. And I'd like to take this opportunity to remind you that this project was always optional. This is not enforced. It is your willingness and your open-mindedness and your own ideas which have helped mould and shape the project, the form it is taking. For I have no vested interest in anyone else understanding these words — as long as you boys grasp the concepts, that is what is important to me.

Because this is not a direct form of mediumship and it is filtered through Brough's mind, you couldn't quite hear the humour behind the statement when I used the term "me." Although I can choose to take form, it is completely unappealing to me, as I am a part of everything and everyone. And I can experience existence on levels above your current ability to imagine.

Indeed, I did have governance over a series of synchronicities directly affecting time and nature around you. But I was not the only one; I am a part of a vibration of all entities who are aware and on the road home. And our sole purpose is to spread peace and to teach a universal curriculum that will expedite the end to suffering.

You are agents, catalysts, of peace. And we are most impressed with the wisdom that you have come to, finding the ability to laugh and the ability to stop taking life too seriously. Because it is so natural to you, you may not realize that this is something that many souls in your world endeavour an entire lifetime to achieve. Sometimes they are only able to emulate it.

And Brough has often referred to certain individuals in the New Age community as Cheshire cats — a wonderful image from *Alice in Wonderland*, where the cat has an unnerving smile on its face constantly. It is the belief of some that, as long as you project positivity, regardless of whether you truly feel it within you or not, that is all that matters. But again, this is simply the folly of materialism. Worrying more about what others see about you but not paying nearly enough attention to actually getting to your destination first.

Always remember to laugh and smile when it feels true, when it feels real, to try not to force anything. For this is one of the laws behind why we say not to change anyone, because indeed, you cannot force the petals of a flower to open — it would kill the flower. You must allow things to happen naturally. So have compassion for those who are not yet ready to progress.

But be aware that people who resist progression are very dangerous in the physical form. And the only kind of healthy intolerance in your world will arrive when people become intolerant of hatred, the infliction of suffering, and the propagation of bigotry and pain on others. And when enough people stand up against those who would enforce hate, malice, and war, that is when your world will change.

Never make the mistake of thinking it is somehow open-minded to allow people to cause destruction of others, to willfully subjugate others. For there is a form of healthy repression — that is to repress and stand up against those who project disharmony.

It may seem like an oxymoron, it may seem like a contradiction in terms, but in order to escape the cosmic programming, the duality that is the fabric of the universe in which you appear to exist right now, you must, to some degree, use its own programming against itself. You must find loopholes. That is why most spiritual teachings do seem to be at some time, from some vantage point, riddled with contradiction.

Of course, not all mysteries will be solved by these chapters, by this particular manuscript. But with dedication and commitment, which you have demonstrated, there is no answer that cannot be uncovered, no mystery that cannot be solved. For those who belong to the camp of progression, mysteries are very unpalatable. Indeed, discovery is your mandate. And is it not true that all of humanity is fundamentally driven by the pursuit of discovery and knowledge?

www.ingramcontent.com/pod-product-compliance
Lightning Source LLC
Chambersburg PA
CBHW031424150426
43191CB00006B/391